Magic Moments Yankees

Magic Moments Yankees

Phil Pepe

TRIUMPH
BOOKS

Babe Ruth, in a quiet moment at Ebbets Field, prior to an early season exhibition game against the Brooklyn Dodgers in 1933.

Outfielders Roger Maris and Mickey Mantle pose for a portrait prior to a game at Yankee Stadium in New York in 1961.

Reflecting on the trials and tribulations of a bitterly disappointing season, Yankee skipper Casey Stengel appears weary and blue as he ponders what might have been.

Lou Gehrig (left) and Joe DiMaggio (right) kneel in their Yankee pinstripes.

Library of Congress Cataloging-in-Publication Data

Pepe, Phil.
  Magic moments : Yankees / Phil Pepe.
     p. cm.
  ISBN-13: 978-1-57243-863-7
  ISBN-10: 1-57243-863-0
  1. New York Yankees (Baseball team)--Anecdotes. 2. Baseball
players--United States--History. I. Title.
  GV875.N4P527 2008
  796.357'64097471--dc22

                              2007041149

This book is available in quantity at special discounts for your group or organization. For further information, contact:

Triumph Books
  542 South Dearborn Street
  Suite 750
  Chicago, Illinois 60605
  (312) 939-3330
  Fax (312) 663-3557

Printed in U.S.A.
ISBN: 978-1-57243-863-7
Design by Wagner | Donovan Design, Inc., Chicago, Illinois

Photos courtesy of:
     Associated Press/World Wide Images 2, 24, 32, 43, 50, 56, 62, 68, 75, 78, 88, 92, 100, 118, 125, 128, 138
     Corbis iv–v, viii–ix, xiv, xvi–xvii, 6, 10, 26, 58, 70, 80, 82, 96, 98, 132, 142, 144, 146–147, 148–149, 150–151,
          154–155, 156
     Getty Images vi–vii, x–xi, 20, 30, 38, 44, 48, 54, 64, 86, 136, 152–153

Contents

Yankee manager Casey Stengel paternally pats the head of pitcher Don Larsen, who tossed a perfect no-hitter against the Dodgers to win the fifth game of the World Series.

Foreword

It's been more than a half century since I had my day in the sun, my one big moment, and people still remember it. Hardly a day goes by that a complete stranger doesn't mention to me that he remembers exactly where he was on that wonderful day, October 8, 1956, and for that I am forever grateful.

Let's face it, if not for that one day, would anybody today know the name Don Larsen?

I have no illusions about my major league career. I didn't have an outstanding career compared to many others, but I was happy to stick around long enough to compile a record of 81–91, with an ERA of 3.78 over 14 years. But I'm proud to have pitched in the major leagues for 14 seasons, for five pennant winners and two World Series champions, and I'm especially proud that for one day I climbed to the top of the mountain—I did what no pitcher in baseball history had done before or since, not Cy Young, not Walter Johnson, not Bob Feller, not Sandy Koufax, not Nolan Ryan, and not Roger Clemens.

Someday, some pitcher may come along and duplicate what I did—pitch a perfect game in the World Series. Whomever he may be, I wish him luck. He's going to be in for a wonderful ride. But know this: While some pitcher may equal what I did, nobody can ever surpass it.

I was privileged to have played in one of baseball's greatest eras, the fifties and sixties, alongside such legendary players as Satchel Paige with the St. Louis Browns; Nellie Fox and Luis Aparicio with the Chicago White Sox; Willie Mays, Willie McCovey, Juan Marichal, Orlando Cepeda, Duke Snider, and Gaylord Perry with the San Francisco Giants; Joe Morgan with the Houston Astros; Brooks Robinson and Jim Palmer with the Baltimore Orioles; and Ernie Banks, Billy Williams, and Ferguson Jenkins with the Chicago Cubs—all Hall of Famers.

And I feel blessed to have played for the New York Yankees, the most prestigious team in sports history, in Yankee Stadium, the cathedral of baseball, for a Hall of Fame manager, Casey Stengel, and with Hall of Fame players Mickey Mantle, Yogi Berra, Phil Rizzuto, and Whitey Ford.

When you think of all the great players who wore the Yankees uniform, the Ruths, Gehrigs, DiMaggios, Mantles, and Jeters, and all the great moments in the team's more than 100-year history—Babe Ruth's 60th home run, Roger Maris's 61st home run, Joe DiMaggio's 56-game hitting streak, Lou Gehrig's 2,130 consecutive games, Reggie Jackson's three home runs in Game 6 of the 1977 World Series, Bucky Dent's home run in the 1978 playoff game against the Boston Red Sox, and so many more, I am flattered that Triumph Books has seen fit to choose my perfect game as the number-one moment in the history of baseball's number-one team.

My career as a major league pitcher might not have been the greatest, but for one day in the fall of 1956, it was perfect.

—Don Larsen

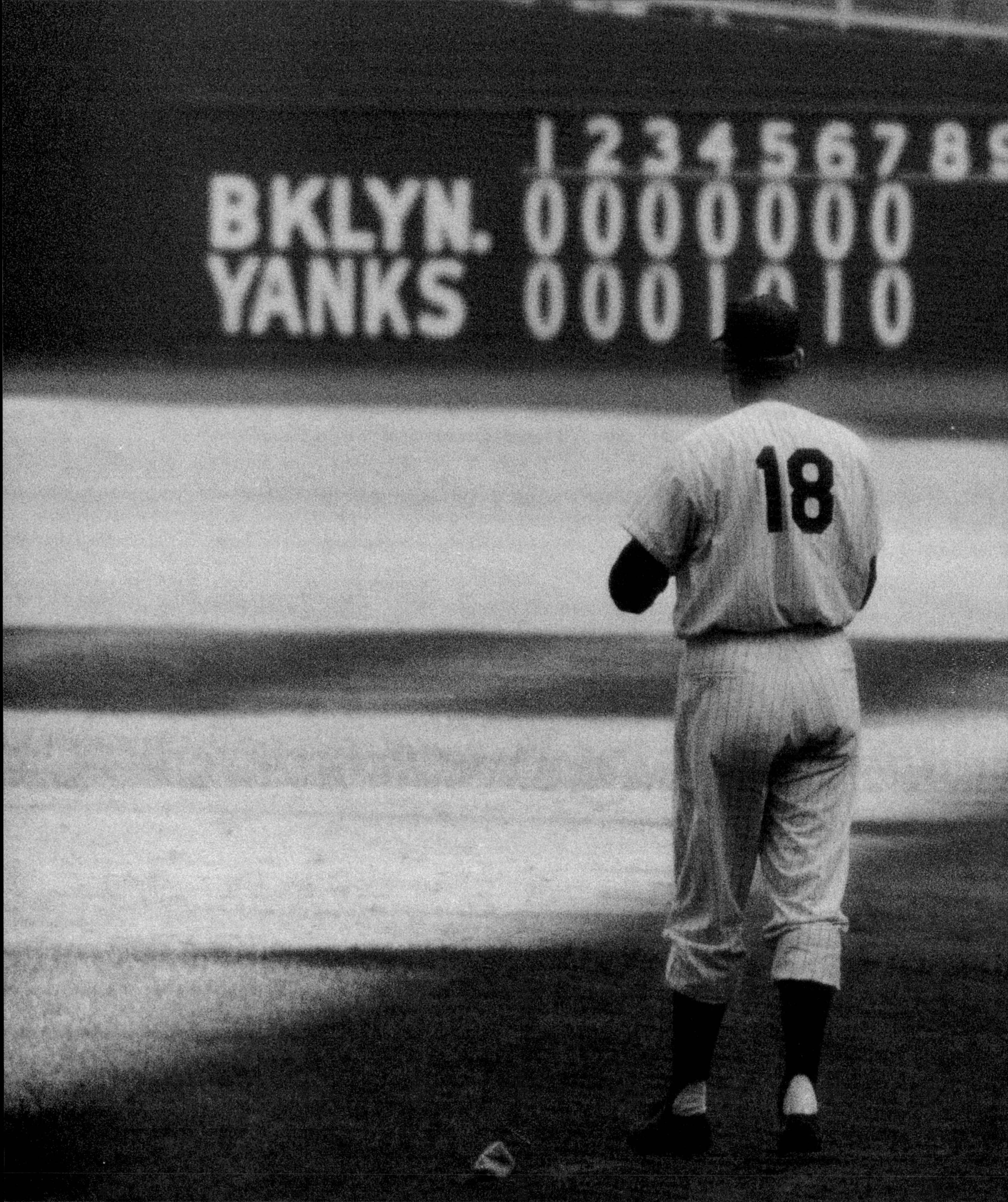
1 2 3 4 5 6 7 8 9
BKLYN. 0 0 0 0 0 0
YANKS
18

Don Larsen studies the scoreboard at Yankee Stadium in the top of the eighth inning as he nears the feat of pitching the first perfect game in World Series history.

Preface

Selecting 40 of the greatest moments in the more than 100-year history of the New York Yankees–the most prestigious, most successful franchise in sports history, winner of 39 American League pennants and 26 World Series–was easy. The hard part was limiting the great moments to only 40.

There are so many choices, so many great stars, so many big games, so many remarkable performances, so many historic events–a kaleidoscope of magic moments.

They range from the team's arrival in New York from Baltimore in 1903 to the procession of 4 million fans pouring through the turnstiles in 2005, from the purchase of Babe Ruth to the free-agent signing of Reggie Jackson, from the construction of Yankee Stadium in 1923 to its reconstruction a half-century later.

They run the gamut from Ruppert to Steinbrenner, Babe to Bucky, Gehrig to Guidry, Mantle to Munson, Joltin' Joe to Reggie Jackson, and Jeter to Jeffrey Maier.

They encompass the memorable hits–home runs by Chris Chambliss, Bucky Dent, Aaron Boone, and Jim Leyritz. The unforgettable games–Reggie Jackson's three home runs in the 1977 World Series, Ron Guidry's 18 strikeouts against the California Angels in 1978, Don Larsen's perfect game in the 1956 World Series, Tony Lazzeri's 11 RBIs in 1936, Lou Gehrig's four home runs in one game in 1932. And the spectacular seasons–Ruth's 60 home runs in 1927, Roger Maris's 61 home runs in 1961, Joe DiMaggio's 56-game hitting streak in 1941, Mickey Mantle's Triple Crown in 1956.

Armed with this knowledge and viewing it with the perspective of the last 100 years, how does one choose the number-one moment in Yankees history?

Is it the purchase of Ruth? The arrival of Casey Stengel? The return of Billy Martin?

Is it Gehrig's 2,130th consecutive game? His farewell speech?

Is it Ruth's 60th home run? Maris's 61st?

Is it the Yankees' first world championship? Their record five consecutive world championships from 1949 to 1953 under Stengel? The four world titles in five years (1996–2000) under Joe Torre?

Is it Ruth's "called shot"? Mantle's titanic home runs off Chuck Stobbs and Bill Fischer? The pine-tar game?

Is it Martin's mad dash and knee-high catch of Jackie Robinson's pop fly to save Game 7 of the 1952 World Series? Derek Jeter's mad dash and flip against Oakland in the 2001 American League divisional series? Jeter's head-first dive into the seats against the Red Sox? Graig Nettles's defensive wizardry in the 1978 World Series?

Is it Allie Reynolds's two no-hitters in one season? Don Mattingly hitting home runs in eight consecutive games? Mattingly's six grand slams in one season? The "Boston Massacre" of 1978?

Great moments come and go; records are made and broken.

Ruth's 60th home run was surpassed by Maris's 61st, which was surpassed by Mark McGwire's 70th, which was surpassed by Barry Bonds' 73rd.

Gehrig's iron-man streak of consecutive games was eclipsed by Cal Ripken Jr.

Chambliss's walk-off home run to win the 1976 American League pennant was at least equaled by Jackson's three blasts on three consecutive pitches against the Dodgers in Game 6 of the 1977 World Series, Dent's dramatic home run against the Red Sox in the 1978 playoff game, Leyritz's three-run homer against the Braves in the 1996 World Series,

Boone's walk-off eleventh-inning home run to beat the Red Sox in the 2003 ALCS, and game-tying, ninth-inning home runs by Tino Martinez and Scott Brosius in back-to-back games in the 2001 World Series.

DiMaggio's milestone consecutive-game hitting streak was not one moment, but a daily soap opera with 56 dramatic, nerve-jangling episodes.

However, for one day, one game, one moment, nothing in Yankees history overshadows one October afternoon in Yankee Stadium in 1956, Game 5 of the World Series between the Yankees and the Brooklyn Dodgers.

To that point, 306 World Series games had been played, and never had there been a no-hitter pitched in any of them. But on October 8, 1956, a 27-year-old journeyman pitcher who had won only 11 games that season, only 30 in his major league career, and who would win only 51 more games over the next 10 years, pitched the first no-hitter in World Series history. Not just a no-hitter, but also a perfect game.

It was improbable. It was unprecedented. It was unpredictable. And a half-century and almost 300 more World Series games later, it remains unmatched.

That's why, in my view, Don Larsen's perfect game is the number-one magic moment in the more than 100-year history of the New York Yankees.

—**Phil Pepe**

40 Magical Moments

Yogi Berra congratulates
Don Larsen on his perfect game.

1 Perfect

As he entered Yankee Stadium on the morning of October 8, 1956, Don Larsen had no idea he was walking into baseball history. He didn't even imagine he would have a chance.

Approaching his locker in the home-team club-house, Larsen was surprised to see a brand-new, game-ready baseball sitting in his left spiked shoe, a practice followed ritualistically by Frank Crosetti, the team's venerable third-base coach, symbolizing the fact that Larsen had been selected to be that day's starting pitcher for the Yankees in Game 5 of the World Series. It was a decision that was as illogical as it was surprising.

The Yankees had obtained Larsen in the winter of 1954, part of a mammoth 18-player trade with the Baltimore Orioles that took 13 days to complete. In two seasons with the Orioles (née St. Louis Browns), Larsen had won 10 games and lost 33, but in New York, he benefited from better offensive and defensive support and from a change in his pitching motion.

Suspecting that he was tipping off his pitches to opposing hitters, the Yankees convinced Larsen to adopt a no-wind-up delivery, which he used to compile a 20–7 record in his first two seasons in New York. At age 27, and possessed of a strong right arm that generated an exploding fastball, Larsen was thought by the Yankees to be a future star, a top-of-the-rotation pitcher, if only he could control his wildness on and off the playing field.

Nicknamed "Goony Bird" for his often-bizarre behavior and because he was a gangly 6'4" and had ears that stuck out from beneath his baseball cap, Larsen's nocturnal forays were the stuff of legend. In St. Petersburg that spring, he was discovered at 5:30 one morning with his car wrapped around a telephone pole. The car was totaled. Larsen was wrecked, but uninjured.

"The man was either out too late or up too early," observed his manager, Casey Stengel.

As the Yankees coasted to the 1956 American League pennant, Stengel carefully set up his pitching rotation for the World Series against the Dodgers, who had finally ended their World Series championship drought and their inability to overcome the Yankees by beating their intercity rivals the previous fall.

A strong regular-season finish had left Larsen with a record of 11–5, prompting Stengel to tab him to start Game 2, after Whitey Ford and ahead of Johnny Kucks and Tom Sturdivant, both of whom had won more games than Larsen during the season.

Larsen hardly inspired confidence with his Game 2 start. Inexplicably, his wildness returned. He walked two batters in the first inning but came away unscathed by getting Jackie Robinson to hit into an inning-ending double play.

A run in the first and a five-run explosion in the second, capped off by Yogi Berra's grand slam, gave Larsen a 6–0 lead heading into the bottom of the second. But a single, an error, a walk, a sacrifice fly, and another walk was as much as Stengel wanted to see. He replaced Larsen with Kucks, who was replaced by Tommy Byrne, as the Dodgers scored six runs to tie the game.

Larsen had pitched only an inning and two-thirds, had allowed just one hit, but walked four and was charged with four runs, a performance that he thought might banish him for the remainder of the Series to the bullpen, or beyond.

After losing the first two games in Brooklyn, the Yankees returned to Yankee Stadium to win Games 3 and 4, so the Series was tied, two games each, going into the pivotal fifth game.

Sportswriters and fans alike speculated on Stengel's choice for his starting pitcher in Game 5. He had a couple of options: Kucks, an 18-game winner who had pitched two innings in relief in Games 1 and 2; and "Bullet" Bob

Turley, who had come with Larsen to the Yankees in the trade with Baltimore. Because of his Game 2 meltdown, not many thought Larsen would get the call, including Larsen himself. Perhaps because Larsen was the Yankees' pitcher with the most rest, or perhaps because of a hunch, Stengel made Larsen his questionable choice.

Dodgers manager Walter Alston countered with Sal "the Barber" Maglie, who was enjoying a resurgence at age 39. Once a notorious Dodger-killer as a member of the New York Giants and public enemy number one among Dodgers fans, Maglie had joined the Dodgers on May 15 of that year, and he proceeded to help his old nemesis win the National League pennant by winning 13 games, including the first no-hitter of his career. He had started Game 1 of the World Series and outpitched Ford in a 6–3 Dodgers victory. Now Maglie was expected to pitch the Dodgers one win away from their second straight World Series triumph.

In stark contrast to his previous start in Game 2, Larsen came out throwing strikes. Through the first three innings, not only had he not walked a batter, but he also had thrown 32 pitches, 22 of them for strikes. The only thing close to a hit was a line drive off the bat of Jackie Robinson leading off the second inning that glanced off the glove of third baseman Andy Carey and ricocheted to shortstop Gil McDougald, who threw Robinson out by half a step.

Meanwhile, Maglie matched Larsen out for out. When Mickey Mantle batted with two outs in the bottom of the fourth, neither team had had a hit or a base runner: 23 batters up, 23 batters down. Maglie threw Mantle a curve ball that got a little more of home plate than Maglie had planned, and Mantle pulled a line drive that curled around the right-field foul pole just above the 296-foot sign for the game's first hit and first run.

With one out in the top of the fifth, Gil Hodges drove a Larsen fastball on a line toward left-center field, Death Valley in Yankee Stadium. In Brooklyn's Ebbets Field, the ball would have landed deep in the left-field seats. In Yankee Stadium, it appeared to be a certain double in the gap, maybe a triple. But Mantle seemed to outrun the ball.

He caught up with it with his blazing speed and reached across his body, his arm stretched as far as it could, to make a backhanded catch as the ball was descending more than 400 feet away from home plate. Years later, Mantle would call it "maybe the greatest catch I ever made; it certainly was the most important."

When the side was retired, Mantle returned to the Yankees dugout and stopped at the water cooler. He looked up to see Larsen standing next to him.

"Hey, Slick," Larsen said. "Wouldn't it be funny if I pitched a no-hitter?"

Horrified at the defiance of baseball's time-honored superstition that mentioning a no-hitter was sure to jinx the effort, Mantle blared at Larsen, "Get the hell out of here."

In the sixth, the Yankees tacked on another run on a single by Carey, Larsen's sacrifice, and an RBI single by Hank Bauer to make it 2–0.

Larsen continued on his road to baseball immortality through the seventh and eighth innings, retiring every batter. In the ninth, he got Carl Furillo on a fly ball to right and Roy Campanella on a ground ball to second. He was one out away from perfection, with the veteran Dale Mitchell, pinch hitting for Maglie, as the last obstacle. Mitchell had spent his entire career with the Cleveland Indians, for whom he batted .312 over 11 seasons. The Indians had sold him in July to the Dodgers, who wanted his veteran presence, his experience, and his productive bat as a pinch-hitter in the pennant push and the World Series–for situations exactly like this. In 19 games with the Dodgers, he had batted a respectable .292.

Larsen's first pitch to Mitchell was a ball, followed by a called strike, a swinging strike, and a foul into the left-field seats. On Larsen's next pitch, his 97th of the game, Mitchell tried to check his swing. Home-plate umpire Babe Pinelli of the National League raised his fist, calling Mitchell out. Mitchell argued, to no avail, that the pitch was high and outside, a ball. Pinelli, umpiring behind home plate for the last time in his career, vehemently disagreed. The call stood. It was Larsen's seventh strikeout of the game. He had faced 27 batters and retired them all. He had pitched his way into baseball immortality.

Writing in the *New York Daily News*, the lead on Joe Trimble's game story the next day read: "The imperfect man pitched a perfect game yesterday."

On NBC television, announcer Vince Scully called it the greatest game ever pitched in baseball history.

Larsen would spend 10 more years in the major leagues with the Yankees, Athletics, White Sox, Giants, Astros, Orioles, and Cubs. In those 10 seasons, he would post a record of 51–51, pitch 14 complete games and six shutouts, and never come close to repeating what he had achieved on the afternoon of October 8, 1956.

Almost 50 years after his masterpiece, Larsen remained bewildered by his unparalleled performance.

"Sometimes," he said, "I wonder why it happened to me."

Roger Maris proves records were made to be broken.

2. 61*

In fact, there never was an asterisk—not then, not now, not ever.

There was, however, a refusal to accept a career .257 hitter as the one to break baseball's most cherished record, an attempt to discredit the latest pursuer as a pretender to the home-run crown, to stonewall, before the fact, any challenge at that record.

It was a record—Babe Ruth's 60 home runs in 1927—that had stood for 34 years, that many thought would never be broken, that had withstood assaults from such vaunted, bona fide sluggers as Jimmie Foxx, Hank Greenberg, and Hack Wilson. But now this .257 hitter, this Roger Maris, a 26-year-old left-handed batter who had hit just 97 home runs in four major league seasons, never more than 39 home runs in any one season, was threatening to erase the sanctified name of Babe Ruth from the record books.

And so it came to pass that on a warm summer afternoon, members of the media convened in the office of baseball commissioner Ford C. Frick, who, not coincidentally, had been a baseball writer himself years before, and Ruth's ghostwriter. The purpose of the gathering was to glean from Frick how baseball would handle the event should someone hit more than 60 home runs in a season. It was a question raised because that year the American League had expanded from eight teams to 10, and the schedule had been increased from 154 games to 162, thereby giving an American League player an additional eight games in which to surpass any other record.

Frick decreed that in order to erase Ruth's home-run mark from the books, a player would have to pass him within 154 games. Should a player exceed Ruth's record of 60 home runs after the 154-game deadline, it would be noted with a "distinguishing mark," signifying that the usurper did so in an expanded season.

"You mean an asterisk?" one writer asked.

"That's right," replied Frick, who never actually uttered the word asterisk. Nevertheless, some baseball writers incorporated the word in their stories, and the phrase took hold.

There had been no early signs in 1961, and nothing in his brief major league history, to foreshadow Maris as a threat to Ruth's record. Maris had come to the Yankees the previous season in a trade with the Kansas City Athletics as a left-handed power hitter whose stroke was tailor-made for Yankee Stadium's short right-field fence, just 296 feet down the line. In his first season as a Yankee, Maris hit 39 home runs, 11 fewer than he had hit in his first three years combined and one fewer than his teammate, Mickey Mantle, the league leader.

Maris did not hit his first home run in 1961 until the Yankees' 11th game. In that game, Mantle belted his sixth and seventh homers. By the time Maris hit his second homer six games later, Mantle, his more popular, more respected, and, to most, more deserving teammate, had hit eight.

In mid-May, Maris's home-run bat started smoking, and home runs started coming in bunches. He hit 10 in 14 games, but it wasn't until he belted number 14 in the Yankees' 44th game on June 2 that he drew even with Mantle. At that point, the newspapers were paying more attention to the terrific tandem, dubbing them the "M&M Boys," than they were to any assault on Ruth's record.

Through June and July, Mantle and Maris were on fire, a dynamic duo of power, their individual and friendly rivalry—they even shared an apartment in Queens with a third member of the team, Bob Cerv—inspiring each other. At the All-Star break, Maris had 33 homers, Mantle 29.

Mantle went on a home-run tear in July and early August. When he belted three in a doubleheader against the Twins on August 6, it gave him 43 for the season, putting him 24 games ahead of Ruth's pace but only two home runs ahead of Maris.

On the day after Mantle's three-homer binge, Maris bunted for a base hit, raising eyebrows but winning a game. Was this any way to chase Babe Ruth?

"I guess that shows you he's not greedy," said manager Ralph Houk. "He must not have been thinking of the record. He must have been thinking of winning."

"I told you this game isn't all made up of home runs," Maris said. "Bunts count, too. If they're going to play back, I'm going to bunt. You put a man on third base, and I don't care if I have the hottest bat in the league. My job is to try to score him."

On August 13, Maris completed a four-game series in Washington in which he went on a homer-a-game diet to draw even with Mantle at 45. They were 16 games ahead of Ruth.

The possibility of breaking the record was mentioned to Maris.

"Don't ask me about that [bleeping] record," he exploded. "I don't want to talk about it. All I'm interested in is winning the pennant."

On September 2, Maris hit two home runs against the Tigers, his 52nd and 53rd. Mantle, with 48, had suffered a pulled muscle in his left forearm. He refused to sit, but the injury cost him some of his power and perhaps a home run or two.

Eight days later, the count was Maris 56, Mantle 53, both still with a legitimate chance at catching Ruth within the 154-game limit prescribed by Frick (they had nine games left to reach 154) or in 162 games. Within days, Mantle's chances had vanished. Suffering with the flu, he went to a doctor for a flu shot and apparently was injected with a contaminated needle. He developed an abscess in his hip that caused him excruciating pain and left him sidelined for several days.

Mantle would hit just one more home run for the remainder of the season, leaving Maris to chase the record alone.

"I'm finished, Rog," Mantle told his friend. "I can't make it. It's up to you."

Of all the players who could have been tapped to challenge baseball's most legendary and most revered record, Roger Maris was among the least likely. He never sought the spotlight, didn't want it, and didn't know how to handle it when he got it. He was a simple man of simple tastes and a simple lifestyle. He was a devoted family man, not a flamboyant man-about-town, a private person, not a celebrity, a blue-collar baseball player, not a poster-boy hero.

Chasing Ruth's record seemed to chip away at Maris's persona rather than enhance it. To many he was unworthy to stand alongside the great Babe: an ingrate, an upstart, a pretender to the great man's throne. Ruth, and the record, it was decided, would have been better served had Mantle challenged it.

But Maris was the chosen one, and the stress of the chase was so intense, it caused patches of his hair to fall out.

Home run number 58 came on September 17 in Detroit in the twelfth inning of the Yankees' 152nd game, leaving Maris three games in which to tie Ruth under Frick's edict (there had been a tie in April that would be replayed and would count as part of the 154-game schedule). Two days later, the Yankees played a doubleheader in Baltimore. Maris batted nine times, walked once, singled, and was victimized by a stiff wind from Hurricane Ethel blowing in from right field that held up several of his drives. There was one game left in the Frick deadline, and Maris needed two home runs to tie Ruth, three to break the record.

"You'd be a Houdini if you did it," Maris said.

He was no Houdini, but Maris gave it his best shot. He leaned into a Milt Pappas fastball in the first inning. On a normal night, it would have reached the seats, but the stiff wind was still whipping in from right field and it held the ball up at the fence. In his second at-bat, Maris got into another fastball, this time driving it through the wind, into the right-field seats.

"As I went around the bases," Maris said later, "I was thinking, 'That's 59.' I had two, maybe three more shots at it."

In his third time at bat, Maris struck out. In his fourth at-bat, he had two close calls: a long drive that had the distance but hooked foul, and another that was knocked down by the wind and caught at the fence.

There would be one more chance in the ninth inning, but it would come against the veteran knuckleball pitcher, Hoyt Wilhelm, and Maris would rather hit against the hardest-throwing left-hander in the league than face a knuckleball. He took the first pitch for strike one. On the second pitch, Maris tried to check his swing, but the ball hit his bat and trickled back to the mound.

Maris had failed to hit 60 home runs in the prescribed 154-games plus one tie, but it wasn't over.

"My season is 162 games," he said.

Maris failed to hit a home run in his next three games, then connected against Jack Fisher of the Orioles for number 60 in the third inning of the Yankees' 159th game. He had tied Babe Ruth, even if it would not be officially recognized. Still, he had hit as many home runs in one season as any player in major league history.

The day after he tied the record, Maris went to Houk's office.

"I'm beat, Ralph," Maris said. "I need a day off."

"You can't take a day off," Houk pleaded. "You're going for the record."

"I can't stand it anymore," Maris argued.

"What should I tell the press?" Houk asked.

"Tell them I went fishing."

Maris sat out game number 160 and failed to hit a home run in his next two games. That brought him to the final game of the season, game number 163 because of the early season tie, still with 60 home runs, still tied with Ruth, officially or unofficially. Maris had one game remaining to become baseball's all-time single-season home-run champion.

Sunday, October 1, 1961, came up a bright and sunny afternoon in the Bronx. With a chance to witness baseball history, only 23,124 showed up at Yankee Stadium. The Boston Red Sox were in town, and Tracy Stallard, a hard-throwing right-hander, the kind of pitcher Maris usually blistered, was on the mound for Boston.

In his first at-bat, Maris was fooled by a change-up and popped up softly to left field.

Maris came to bat for the second time in the fourth inning. Phil Rizzuto was announcing the game on television. This was his call:

"Here comes Roger Maris. They're standing up, waiting to see if Roger is going to hit number 61. Here's the windup…the pitch to Roger…way outside, ball one. The fans are starting to boo…low, ball two…that one was in the dirt…and the boos get louder.… Two balls, no strikes on Roger Maris.… Here's the windup…fastball…*hit deep to right…this could be it…holy cow…he did it…61 home runs.…*"

In January 1920, Babe Ruth sat down with Colonel Jacob Ruppert and signed on to play for the Yankees.

3. I Got You, Babe

It was a match made in heaven–George Herman Ruth and New York. The brash, bold, boisterous, braggadocios Babe, known for his booming bat and his nocturnal forays, in the world's greatest metropolis, the center of commerce, industry, communications, and bright lights; the insatiable insomniac in the city that never sleeps–and it changed the face of baseball forever.

The deal was consummated with a contract of sale signed on the day after Christmas, 1919, and the transfer from the New York Yankees to Harry Frazee, owner of the Boston Red Sox, of a check in the amount of $25,000. The formal announcement of the transaction would not come until January 5, 1920.

Under terms of the agreement, the Yankees would send Frazee three additional payments of $25,000, establishing the sale price at $100,000, twice as much as ever had been paid for any other player. In addition, Colonel Jacob Ruppert, owner of the Yankees, agreed to a loan of $300,000 to Frazee, guaranteeing the latter's mortgage on Fenway Park.

Why would Frazee agree to sell, at any price, baseball's greatest star, its biggest attraction? Only 24 years old, Ruth was already hailed by most as the best left-handed pitcher in the American League, having won 23 games for the Red Sox in 1916 and 24 in 1917. In addition, the mighty Babe had become the most feared and most powerful batter in the game. Recognizing his prowess as a hitter, the Red Sox began shuttling him between the pitcher's mound and the outfield. In 1918, he won 13 games as a pitcher and led the league in home runs with 11. The following year, his role as an outfielder escalating, he won nine game as a pitcher and hit the unheard-of total of 29 home runs, 19 more than the league runner-up and more than any other player had ever hit in a season in the game's history.

This was the Babe Ruth that the Yankees coveted.

The story handed down through the years, probably apocryphal, is that Frazee needed the money to finance his Broadway production, *No, No, Nanette*. While the theater was the first love of Frazee, a transplanted New Yorker, there were other factors. He needed the money to avoid defaulting on Fenway Park mortgage payments, and he had grown weary of Ruth's demands for more money and the Babe's off-field shenanigans.

While the city of New York in general, and Yankees fans in particular, were ecstatic with the news of the acquisition of the mighty Babe, Ruth himself was less than enthusiastic.

"When the Yankees score eight runs in the first inning and slowly pull away." —Yankees owner Colonel Jacob Ruppert, when asked what he considered a perfect day at the ballpark

---

When the deal was announced, Ruth was spending the off-season in California, playing a series of exhibition games, golfing, and partying. Informed of the sale, Ruth was hardly warm to the idea of pulling up stakes. He professed his love for the Boston area, for the great Red Sox fans, for his farm in suburban Sudbury, and for his new business venture, a cigar factory.

Perhaps Ruth was merely campaigning for a new contract. He still had two years remaining on his three-year, $10,000-per-year deal with the Red Sox. If he were to go to New York, Ruth insisted, he would have to have a new contract with a substantial raise. He even asked for a percentage of the sale price. The Yankees agreed to pay Ruth the munificent sum of $20,000 for 1920. Ruth dropped his demand for a percentage of the sale price, and the Babe's attitude toward going to New York changed abruptly. He proclaimed his approval of the deal, said he was excited about coming to New York, and vowed his dedication to his new team.

Ruth met up with his new teammates in Penn Station on February 28 for the train trip to Jacksonville for spring training, where the newcomer was the center of attention. An expanded press corps of 13 reporters was in camp to chronicle the Babe's every move, and he gave them ample copy for the stories they sent back to their newspapers.

The newest Yankee was less than a smashing success in spring training. He wasn't hitting, and fans rode him unmercifully. One in particular was so vociferous, Ruth went into the stands after him.

Ruth maintained that "spring training don't mean nothing," and when reporters asked him if he thought he could match his 1919 total of 29 home runs, the Babe boldly bellowed, "I'll hit 50 this year."

It was an outrageous boast. No team, much less an individual player, in either league had hit 50 home runs the previous season. The Yankees had led the major leagues with 45 homers.

Ruth's first game as a Yankee came on April 16 in Shibe Park, Philadelphia. He had asked manager Miller Huggins to allow him to play center field because he was concerned about injuring himself by running into walls in left or right. Huggins complied. But in center field, Ruth dropped a fly ball, allowing the Athletics to score two runs that beat the Yankees. At bat, Babe stroked a pair of singles.

In the home opener at the Polo Grounds a week later, Ruth pulled a rib-cage muscle after batting once and left the game. It was not an auspicious debut for the big man, who did not hit his first home run until May 1, the Yankees' 12th game. After that first one, Ruth's home runs came in bunches. He hit 12 in the month of May, 12 more in June.

On July 15, in the Yankees' 83rd game, just six games past the midpoint in the season, he hit his 29th home run, matching his major league record set the previous year.

On August 4, Ruth had 37 homers and a 26-game hitting streak that hiked his batting average to a season-high .391.

"I had a better year than Hoover."
—Babe Ruth, when a reporter pointed out that Ruth's demand for an $80,000 salary in 1930 was $5,000 more than President Herbert Hoover was paid

---

Ruth's home-run production slowed in August. He hit only seven in five weeks, but he finished strong, with 10 home runs in his final 24 games.

His 54 home runs were astounding. George Sisler, second in the American League, had 19. The National League champion, Cy Williams of Philadelphia, hit 15. Babe's 54 homers were more than any other team except the Phillies, who hit 64.

While Ruth's home-run heroics could not save the Yankees from a second straight third-place finish, three games behind Cleveland, his presence, and his booming bat, were a boon at the box office as the Yankees surpassed the 1 million mark in home attendance for the first time, drawing 1,289,422, more than double their previous year's total. Ruth had paid for himself and justified his huge salary.

It wouldn't be long before Ruth's bat began to produce championships. In their first 17 years in New York, the Yankees (née Highlanders) had failed to win a pennant and finished higher than fourth place only twice. In Ruth's second season in New York, the Yankees won their first American League pennant, and they would win seven pennants and four World Series in his 15 years with the team.

The mighty Ruth's contribution to baseball and the Yankees was more than just championships, home runs, and increased attendance. When he arrived in New York, the game was reeling from the 1919 Black Sox Scandal, in which eight members of the Chicago White Sox were brought to trial for conspiring to throw the World Series to the Cincinnati Reds and banned from the game for life by the commissioner of baseball, Judge Kenesaw Mountain Landis.

Public confidence in the integrity of the game was at an all-time low. Suspicion and skepticism abounded. The game needed a savior, and Babe Ruth was the perfect angel of mercy. His booming home runs and his bombastic behavior gave the game a larger-than-life hero that fans could embrace.

Ruth was part of a golden era of sports, a time when the names Jack Dempsey, Red Grange, Johnny Longden, Bobby Jones, and Bill Tilden were magic. But Ruth was the greatest hero of them all. He hit the most and the longest home runs, ate the most hot dogs, drank the most beer, had the flashiest cars, was seen with the most dazzling women, wore the most fashionable clothes, had the most prodigious appetite, the heartiest laugh, the most

booming voice, the biggest belly, and the skinniest legs. And he saved baseball.

When the game needed a hero, a savior, George Herman Ruth stepped in to accept the role, capturing the imagination of a public that had become suspicious, that had grown disillusioned, that felt betrayed. Babe Ruth was the right man at the right time. He may have been the only man who could save baseball, who could capture the fancy of a skeptical American public.

His name blared from newspaper headlines almost daily. Italian Americans in New York loved baseball, and they loved Babe Ruth. "The Bambino," they called him, using the Italian word for *baby*, and the nickname stuck.

Stories about Ruth soon became legendary. He was assigned to room with veteran outfielder Ping Bodie, and when reporters, constantly in search of new stories about the Babe, inquired how it was rooming with a hero, Bodie replied, "I don't know. I never see him. I room with his suitcase."

Joe DiMaggio goes on a hitting streak that still remains baseball's oldest major individual record.

"I'd walk into the owner's office, stick out my hand, and say, 'Hiya partner.'"
—Joe DiMaggio, when asked what he'd be paid if he played in the 1990s, when baseball players' salaries had skyrocketed

4 Streak

Joe DiMaggio was in a slump.

He had started the 1941 season by hitting safely in each of his first eight games, but on the morning of Thursday, May 15, DiMaggio found himself in a horrendous three-week slump during which his average plummeted more than 200 points.

"I'm lunging and hitting some on the handle," he told reporters.

As they prepared to face the Chicago White Sox, the Yankees had lost four straight, seven of their last nine, and had tumbled five-and-a-half games out of first place. A frightening trend was being established.

Now, before a sparse crowd of 9,040, on this hazy afternoon in Yankee Stadium, DiMaggio, who was hitless in his previous game, stroked a solid single to center field off left-hander Edgar Smith to drive in Phil Rizzuto. It was not the end of DiMaggio's slump, his only hit of the day, and it was ineffectual and inconsequential in light of other events. The big news of the day was the release of the fabled Dizzy Dean by the Chicago Cubs.

Despite DiMaggio's single, the Yankees lost, 13–1, and his average dipped another two points to .304. But like a drop of rain in Johnstown, a crack in the sidewalk on a street in San Francisco, and a misstep by Mrs. O'Leary's cow in Chicago, this single in the Bronx was the start of something.

If the great streak had a modest beginning, it followed that pattern in its early days, hardly causing a ripple in the baseball waters. Although he hit safely in each of the next 12 games, only four times did he have a multiple-hit game. It wasn't until game 14 of the streak, in Washington on May 29, that the newspapers began to pay attention to what DiMaggio was doing, and then only in light of other events.

It was a hot, humid day, the barometer rising steadily, and the threat of rain hanging in the heavy air. Rain was imminent when Tommy Henrich homered in the top of the fifth to put the Yankees ahead of the Washington Senators, 2–1. The Senators tied the score in the bottom of the inning, sending the game into the sixth, when the Yankees batted around, breaking the game wide open. But the heavens finally burst with a thunderstorm that rendered the field unplayable. The game was halted; everything that had happened in the sixth inning was eradicated with the official records reverting to the fifth.

All batting records were official, although the score was recorded as a 2–2 tie.

DiMaggio had singled in the aborted sixth, but that was washed away. Fortunately, Joe D. had stroked a single in the fourth to extend his streak to 14 games. DiMaggio scored on a single by Frank Crosetti, who stretched his hitting streak to 11 games. But first baseman Johnny Sturm was not so fortunate.

Sturm entered the game having hit in 11 consecutive games. He went hitless in the first five innings but singled in the ill-fated sixth. That hit was disallowed, and Sturm's streak was at an end. In calling attention to that unfortunate development, the writers parenthetically mentioned the good fortune of DiMaggio and Crosetti, whose batting streaks were still intact. It was the first mention in print that DiMag was on a hitting streak.

There would be other close calls around which DiMaggio would have to navigate on his journey to baseball history.

In game 16, his only hit was a lazy pop fly that should have been caught but dropped untouched between two outfielders.

In game 30, he got the benefit of the doubt from the official scorer on a routine ground ball in the sixth inning to White Sox shortstop Luke Appling. The ball bounced off Appling's shoulder and trickled a few feet away from the shortstop, who grabbed for the ball, dropped it, picked it up, and fired too late to first base. The scorer ruled it a hit, DiMaggio's only hit of the game.

In game 36, DiMaggio failed to get a hit in his first three at-bats against St. Louis Browns rookie Bob Muncrief. In the bottom of the eighth, DiMaggio prolonged the streak with a single to left field.

"Why didn't you walk DiMaggio the last time to stop him?" Browns manager Luke Sewell asked Muncrief after the game.

"That wouldn't have been fair," Muncrief replied. "To him or me. Hell, he's the greatest player I've ever seen."

In game 38, against the Browns, DiMaggio again failed to hit in his first three at-bats. He was due to hit fourth in the final inning, meaning the Yankees needed one base runner for him to come to bat.

Red Rolfe walked with one out, and Henrich came to bat with DiMaggio on deck. Suddenly, Henrich had a frightening thought.

"What if I hit into a double play?" he wondered. "Joe would not come to bat, and the streak would be over."

Another thought came quickly to Henrich, and he dropped down a perfect bunt, moving Rolfe to second, and DiMaggio was saved a turn at-bat. Today, DiMaggio would have been walked to fill the open base, but they played by different rules in 1941. The Browns pitched to him, and DiMag ripped a double to left.

On June 7 in St. Louis, DiMaggio lashed out three singles to extend his hitting streak to 22 games. Not only was he only halfway to the all-time record, but his wasn't even the longest hitting streak alive in the American League at the time. Starting on May 15, the same day as DiMaggio, Ted Williams of the Boston Red Sox, having played one more game, had hit in 23 straight.

On Sunday, June 8, both the Yankees and the Red Sox played doubleheaders, New York in St. Louis, Boston in Chicago. While Williams was horse-collared (0-for-5, with four walks), DiMaggio homered twice and drove in four runs

in the first game of his doubleheader, doubled and knocked in three runs in the second game. He had increased his streak to 24 games, and shaken off the mighty Williams.

"I certainly was conscious of my streak," Williams said in later years. "And DiMaggio's was just starting to get into the papers then. I went to Chicago with 23 games and did a big and glorious zero, and Joe carried on."

Carry on he did. A single in game 25, a single and homer in game 26, another homer in game 27, singles in each of the next three games. On June 21, DiMaggio singled against Detroit to extend his streak to 34 games, passing Rogers Hornsby's National League record.

One week later, on June 28, the Yankees met the Philadelphia Athletics in Shibe Park. The Yankees pounded out 14 hits for a 7–4 victory that moved them into first place. Charlie Keller's home run in the seventh extended the Yankees' record of having hit at least one homer in 23 consecutive games. They would take the home-run streak to 25 before it was stopped.

But all the focus was on the individual hitting streak of DiMaggio. With a double in the fourth, he became the fourth player in major league history to hit safely in 40 straight games, tying Ty Cobb's 1911 streak, one behind George Sisler's 19-year-old modern record, and four behind Willie Keeler's all-time mark set in 1897.

The Yankees were scheduled for a doubleheader in Washington on Sunday, June 29, and the prospect of seeing DiMaggio tie and break the modern record on the same day crammed 31,000 into Griffith Stadium despite temperatures that reached 100 degrees. They were not disappointed.

Batting against the baffling knuckleball of Dutch Leonard, DiMaggio lined out to center field in his first at-bat. In his second, Leonard's knuckler fluttered erratically, putting him behind in the count, 3–0. He looked at third-base coach Art Fletcher for a sign and got the go-ahead to hit.

"I owe a lot to [manager] Joe McCarthy for the streak," Joe would say in later years. "He never gave me the take sign. Always let me take my rips."

With the count 3–0, DiMaggio took his rip but popped up feebly to third.

DiMaggio came to bat for the third time in the sixth inning. On a 1–1 count, Leonard tried to slip a fastball by him. It was a mistake. DiMaggio tagged it on a line to left center, the ball splitting Washington outfielders George Case and Doc Cramer and rocketing to the fence 422 feet away. The partisan Washington crowd erupted as DiMaggio pulled into second base, having tied Sisler's modern record of hitting safely in 41 consecutive games.

Baseball players are a notoriously superstitious lot, and the great DiMaggio was no exception. He would always make certain to touch second base on his way to his defensive position in center field. Imagine his chagrin when he came to bat for the first time in the second game of the doubleheader and discovered his favorite bat, the one he had used through much of the streak, was gone. It had been stolen from the bat rack by a souvenir-hunting fan. DiMaggio was disheartened, but his teammate, Tommy Henrich, came up with a solution. Earlier in the season, Henrich, in a hitting slump, had borrowed a bat from DiMaggio. Henrich came alive with it at the plate. He offered to return DiMaggio's bat "for luck," and DiMaggio accepted.

The lucky bat failed to perform any magic in DiMaggio's first three at-bats. But in the seventh inning he faced Red Anderson, likely his final at-bat of the game. Anderson's first pitch whistled inches from DiMaggio's chin. He jumped back and wordlessly got back into the box, settling himself with his "lucky bat" held high off his right shoulder. On the next pitch, DiMaggio blistered a line drive into left field for a clean hit and the record. Once again, the crowd erupted with an ear-piercing roar.

"They were hanging from the rafters," recalled Senators first baseman Mickey Vernon. "A lot of fans came down from New York to root for Joe and see him break the record. When he tied it, the crowd went wild. Then when he broke the record in the second game, the place went crazy."

Sisler was quick to acknowledge the coronation of a new king of streaks and the end of his record. In a telegram to DiMaggio, Sisler said: "Congratulations. I'm glad a real hitter broke it. Keep going."

Having surpassed Sisler's modern major league record, DiMaggio's next goal was the all-time record of 44 by Wee Willie Keeler. It came on July 1, in the second game of a doubleheader against the Red Sox at Yankee Stadium. Lured by DiMaggio's streak, 52,832 piled into the big ballpark on a hot and humid Tuesday afternoon. DiMaggio extended his streak to 43 games with his third at-bat on a questionable call by the official scorer of a ball that handcuffed Sox third baseman Jim Tabor. As if to take the onus off the scorer, DiMaggio singled cleanly in his next at-bat.

In the second game, he left no suspense for the huge crowd, singling over the head of shortstop Joe Cronin in the first inning to arrive at number 44, thus tying Keeler's unpublicized record.

To surpass Keeler, DiMaggio had to wait only until his third at-bat in game number 45. He had been robbed by right fielder Stan Spence's one-handed stab of a vicious liner in his first at-bat, and bounced to third baseman Tabor in his second. But in the fifth, he drilled a line drive over the left-field fence, a ball hit so viciously it disappeared from view before he had time to admire his record-breaking hit.

"I don't believe anybody but a ballplayer is in a position to appreciate what it means to hit safely in 45 straight games," Yankees manager Joe McCarthy said admiringly.

Said Ted Williams: "I really wish I could hit like that guy DiMaggio. I'm being honest. Joe's big and strong, and he can club the ball without any effort. These hot days I wear myself out laying into it, and I lose seven or eight pounds out there. When it's hot, I lose my snap or something."

At the time, Williams was batting .401.

DiMaggio continued a torrid pace through the early part of July with at least two hits in seven of eight games to arrive at 52 straight without the added pressure of chasing a record. Every game merely extended his own record.

Now, newspapers not only reported the extension of DiMaggio's streak, but the daily question was when would

DiMaggio be stopped, and who would be the one to stop him? Some thought he might extend the streak through the remainder of the season.

On July 17, lured again by the great DiMaggio, 67,468 jammed Cleveland's Municipal Stadium. It was the largest crowd in the major leagues in the 1941 season.

Left-hander Al Smith pitched for Cleveland against DiMaggio's closest friend, the irrepressible Lefty Gomez. But the hero—or villain—of the piece would be Indians third baseman Ken Keltner, acknowledged as the slickest-fielding third baseman in the league.

On his first at-bat, DiMaggio lashed a bullet down the line at third. Keltner speared it with a backhanded stab and threw DiMaggio out at first.

"I couldn't get out of the box quickly because of the rains the day before," DiMaggio remembered, "and Ken's long throw just nipped me."

There would have been no throw if Keltner had not been playing so deep.

"Deep?" DiMaggio said. "My God, he was standing in left field."

On his second at-bat, DiMaggio was walked, and the crowd, pulling hard for the home-team Indians in their struggle to catch the first-place Yankees, nevertheless booed.

When he came to bat in the seventh, DiMaggio noticed that Keltner, still playing deep, had moved another step closer to the foul line. DiMaggio knew he could easily have bunted for a base hit, but his pride would not permit him to take such a wimpish approach to extend the streak.

"He [Keltner] dared me to bunt on him," DiMaggio recalled, "but I didn't bunt during the entire streak." (By contrast, in 1978, Pete Rose had six bunt hits in his 44-game streak.)

Again, DiMaggio hit a wicked smash to third, just inside the line. Keltner hardly had to move to stab it on a short hop and throw DiMaggio out by a step.

When he came to bat in the eighth, Joe faced a new pitcher, reliever Jim Bagby. The Yankees had scored two runs to take a 4–1 lead and had the bases loaded with one out. On a 2–1 fastball, Joe smashed one hard and deep to shortstop, but right at Lou Boudreau. The ball took a nasty hop as Boudreau was about to field it, but the Indians shortstop recovered quickly, snared the ball at shoulder height, and started a short-to-second-to-first double play.

The streak was over, ended at 56 games...but it really isn't over. More than six decades later, it remains baseball's oldest major individual record.

Twelve men have occupied the Oval Office of the White House since DiMaggio's streak. Wars have been fought in Europe and Japan, in Korea and Vietnam, in Iraq and Afghanistan. Two of the four Beatles were born, grew up, met up with two other Beatles, formed a band, invaded the United States, changed the world of music, influenced a generation's dress and style, disbanded, and died since Joe DiMaggio hit in 56 consecutive games.

In 1941, fewer than 8,000 television sets were in use in the United States, movie-goers watched Orson Welles in *Citizen Kane* and Gary Cooper in *Sergeant York*, *Duffy's Tavern* and *Inner Sanctum* were on the radio, Glenn Miller's "Chattanooga Choo-Choo" was on the jukeboxes, a new automobile sold for $850, a gallon of gas for 12¢, and a loaf of bread for 8¢ while DiMaggio was taking dead aim at George Sisler's record of hitting safely in 41 games.

Babe Ruth's presumably unbeatable record of 60 home runs in a season has been surpassed seven times, and his 714 career home runs, Ty Cobb's 4,191 hits, Lou Gehrig's iron-man streak of 2,130 consecutive games, Cobb's 892 stolen bases in a career and 96 in a season, Walter Johnson's 3,508 career strikeouts, and Rube Waddell's 349 strikeouts in a season have all been broken. But DiMaggio's 56-game hitting streak survives.

All the way back to 1893, only 39 players have had hitting streaks of at least 30 games, and only 19 of them have done it in the years since DiMaggio's record streak.

Ted Williams, widely acclaimed as the greatest hitter the game has known, never had a hitting streak of 30 games.

Rod Carew, the best pure hitter since Williams, never had a hitting streak of 30 games.

Tony Gwynn, Henry Aaron, Wade Boggs, and Roberto Clemente, with 19 batting championships among them, never had a hitting streak of 30 games.

The record hitting streak for 13 of the 30 major league teams is fewer than 30 games.

DiMaggio himself, except for his record, never had another streak that reached 30 games.

So the question is raised: Is this one record that will never be broken, as so many historians believe? Given the number of years that have passed without so much as a bona fide challenge to DiMaggio's record, the decline in batting averages over the years, and the ever-changing nature of the game, it is difficult to imagine any player even approaching the record, let alone surpassing it.

The 56-game hitting streak is special. A hitting streak is unique, different from other records. It's suspenseful, like a daily soap opera. It's a high-wire act that can be ended with one false step, one mistake, one bad day. It requires consistency, a strong resolve, and, as DiMaggio himself admitted, a large measure of luck.

"I have said many times that you have to be lucky to keep a hitting streak going," DiMaggio once said. "I was lucky in the Pacific Coast League to go 61 games in 1933, and I had some good fortune in New York in 1941, getting a hit in 56 consecutive games.

"There was, of course, a lot of pressure that built up along the way, especially during the streak with the Yankees. Our manager, Joe McCarthy, was a great help. He never gave me the take sign once. In fact, at times he even gave me the hit sign in situations where the count was three balls and no strikes, something a manager would normally never do at that time under any other circumstances."

Teammate Frank Crosetti remembered a train trip the Yankees took from Washington to Philadelphia during the streak.

"A bunch of us were sitting in the drawing room, including McCarthy," Crow recalled. "Joe [DiMaggio] came by, looked in, saw McCarthy, and stopped to thank him for letting Joe hit 3-and-0. In those days, we never hit 3–0. Nobody. Not even DiMag. McCarthy just said, 'You deserve it.'"

When the streak ended for DiMaggio, he was both relieved and glum.

"Nobody thought he would ever be stopped," said Rizzuto. "We all thought it would just go on. When it ended, the way it ended, it was a shock. After the game, Joe asked me to stay behind. There were a lot of *paisans* in Cleveland, and they were mad that the streak ended. Keltner had to have a police escort to leave the stadium.

"We waited until the crowd was gone, and Joe and I walked back to the Cleveland Hotel. We passed a bar and Joe turned to go in, and I followed him.

"'No, Phil,' he said. 'You go back to the hotel. I want to be alone.'

"So I started walking back to the hotel alone, and I heard him call me.

"'Hey, Phil,' he said. 'I forgot my wallet in the clubhouse. Give me all your money.'

"So I took out my money, all I had, and gave it to him. It came to $14.80. He never paid me back. He just forgot about it. That's how upset he was."

Many years later, Rizzuto reminded DiMaggio that he never paid back the loan, and DiMaggio offered to give him the $14.80.

"Are you kidding?" Rizzuto said. "Nothing doing. It's worth the $14.80 just to be able to tell that story."

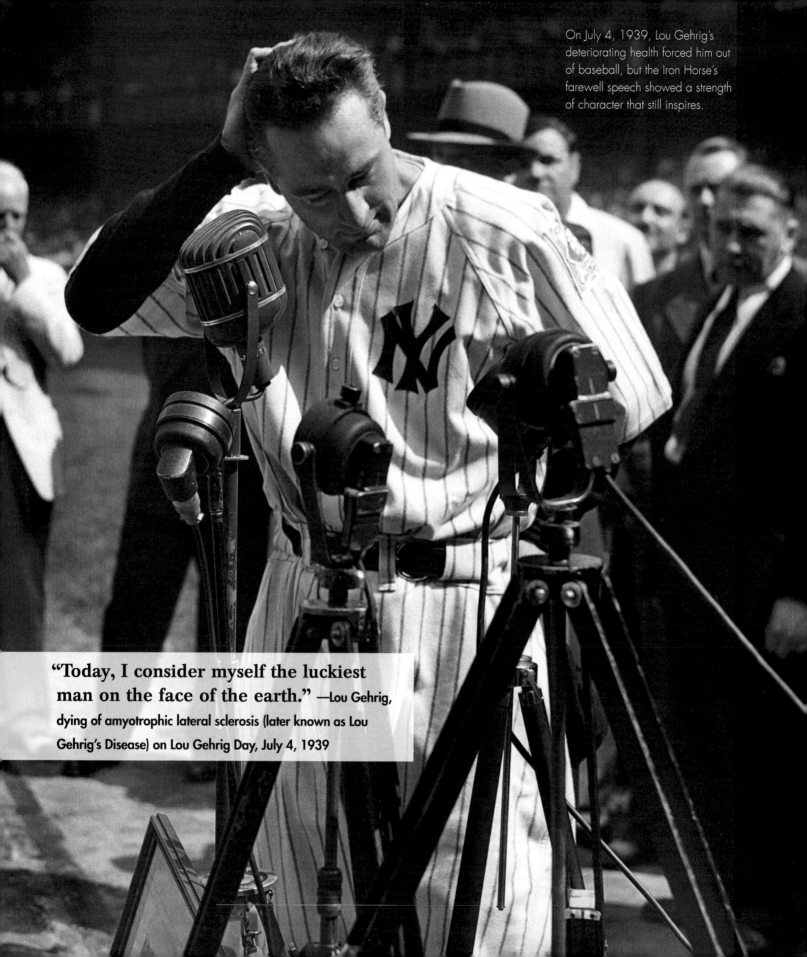

On July 4, 1939, Lou Gehrig's deteriorating health forced him out of baseball, but the Iron Horse's farewell speech showed a strength of character that still inspires.

"Today, I consider myself the luckiest man on the face of the earth." —Lou Gehrig, dying of amyotrophic lateral sclerosis (later known as Lou Gehrig's Disease) on Lou Gehrig Day, July 4, 1939

5. Luckiest Man

Few in the crowd of 61,808, or members of the media, or Yankees players, past and present, who had gathered at Yankee Stadium on that July 4, 1939, knew the truth.

Lou Gehrig was dying.

The famed Iron Horse of baseball, who exuded power and strength, the indestructible man who had ignored broken bones and pulled muscles to play in 2,130 consecutive games, had been afflicted with amyotrophic lateral sclerosis (years later it would become known as Lou Gehrig's Disease), a mysterious ailment that attacked the central nervous system and for which there was no known treatment or cure.

Two months and two days earlier, he had removed himself from the Yankees lineup, ending his incredible streak that had stretched across 15 seasons. A month later, rapidly declining physically, his hair graying swiftly, his body falling apart perceptibly, his accelerated weight loss unable to be reversed, Gehrig had gone to the Mayo Clinic in Rochester, Minnesota, for a series of tests. The diagnosis was made by Dr. Harold C. Habein:

> This is to certify that Mr. Lou Gehrig has been under examination at the Mayo Clinic from June 13 to June 19, 1939, inclusive.
>
> After a careful and complete examination, it was found that he is suffering from amyotrophic lateral sclerosis. This type of illness involves the motor pathways and cells of the central nervous system and in lay terms is known as a form of chronic poliomyelitis (infantile paralysis).
>
> The nature of this trouble makes it such that Mr. Gehrig will be unable to continue his active participation as a baseball player.

The letter was dated June 19, 1939, Gehrig's 36th birthday.

Soon after his return from the Mayo Clinic, the Yankees, at the suggestion of a New York baseball writer, staged Lou Gehrig Appreciation Day at Yankee Stadium, to be conducted between games of a doubleheader against the Washington Senators on the Fourth of July.

All of Gehrig's teammates from the famed Murderers' Row were there, including Wally Pipp, the man Gehrig replaced at first base; Waite Hoyt; Mark Koenig; Bob Meusel; Tony Lazzeri; and the mighty Babe Ruth himself, now four years into retirement.

A World Series banner from 1927 was raised in center field, after which Gehrig, in his Yankees uniform, was showered with gifts. An announcement was made that Gehrig's No. 4 would be officially retired, never to be worn by any other Yankee, the first such tribute in baseball history. At that point, the crowd began to chant: "We want Gehrig…we want Gehrig…."

When it was his turn to speak, Gehrig, his head bowed, staring at the ground in front of him, pulled a handkerchief from his pocket, blew his nose, and wiped his eyes. He was too choked with emotion. The words would not come. Sportswriter Dan Daniel, the day's emcee, stepped to the microphone and told the crowd that Gehrig was too choked up to speak and asked him to thank the fans for him.

At that moment, manager Joe McCarthy sidled up next to Gehrig and whispered in his ear, urging him not to disappoint the fans who had come to honor him. Now Gehrig walked laboriously to the microphone, paused for a few moments as he collected himself, and then addressed the crowd:

> Fans, for the past two weeks you have been reading about the bad break I got. Yet today I consider myself the luckiest man on the face of the earth. I have been in ballparks for 17 years and have never

received anything but kindness and encouragement from you fans.

Look at these grand men. Which of you wouldn't consider it the highlight of his career just to associate with them for even one day?

Sure I'm lucky. Who wouldn't consider it an honor to have known Jacob Ruppert? Also, the builder of baseball's greatest empire, Ed Barrow? To have spent six years with that wonderful little fellow, Miller Huggins? Then to have spent the next nine years with that outstanding leader, that smart student of psychology, the best manager in baseball today, Joe McCarthy?

Sure I'm lucky. When the New York Giants, a team you would give your right arm to beat, and vice versa, sends you a gift–that's something. When everybody down to the groundskeepers and those boys in white coats remember you with trophies–that's something.

When you have a father and a mother who work all their lives so you can have an education and build your body–it's a blessing. When you have a wife who has been a tower of strength and shown more courage than you dreamed existed–that's the finest I know.

So I close in saying I might have had a tough break, but I have an awful lot to live for.

When it was over, there was a thunderous roar from the crowd, and Ruth, to whom Gehrig did not speak for four years over some disagreement between the women in their lives–allegedly remarks between Gehrig's mother and Ruth's wife–walked over to Gehrig, threw a burly arm around Lou's neck, whispered in his ear, and squeezed him in a tender embrace.

Less than two years later, on June 6, 1941, 13 days short of his 38th birthday, Lou Gehrig, baseball's legendary Iron Horse, was dead.

6. Bucky Dents the Sox

The baseball gods had ordained it. They wouldn't have it any other way: the Boston Red Sox and New York Yankees, the game's two most heated rivals, baseball's Hatfields and McCoys, meeting in a one-game, winner-take-all playoff to determine the championship of the American League East and the right to move on to the playoffs and beyond.

How had it come to this? On July 19, 1978, the Yankees were 14 games behind the Red Sox, but they staged a furious second-half rush, caught the Red Sox on September 10, and passed them three days later. On September 16, the Yankees had opened a three-and-a-half-game lead. Now it was the Red Sox's turn to stage a comeback.

They closed the gap to one game on September 23 with eight games remaining, and they remained one game behind until the final day of the season, when Boston beat Toronto, 5–0, and the Yankees lost to Cleveland, 9–2.

At the close of baseball business on October 1, this is how the standings looked in the AL East:

	W	L	Games Behind
New York	99	63	—
Boston	99	63	—

For only the second time in baseball history (Cleveland versus Boston in 1948 was the first), there would be a one-game play-off to decide a championship. It would be played–determined by an earlier coin flip–on Boston's home field, Fenway Park, on Monday afternoon, October 2, 1978.

It was a crisp, cool, sun-drenched New England afternoon as the Yankees and Red Sox prepared to do battle. Ron Guidry, with a record of 24–3, drew the starting pitching assignment for the Yankees. For the Red Sox, it was 16-game winner Mike Torrez, who had pitched and won the decisive sixth game of the 1977 World Series for the Yankees and then signed a free-agent contract with the Red Sox a few weeks later.

Boston scratched out a run off Guidry in the second and another in the sixth, while Yankees bats were stifled by Torrez, who hadn't won a game in six weeks but was being a big-game pitcher once again.

Down 2–0, time was running out for the Yankees as they batted in the seventh. With one out, Chris Chambliss and Roy White hit consecutive singles, but pinch-hitter Jim Spencer flied out for the second out. That brought up Bucky Dent, the Yankees' ninth-place hitter who was hitless for the day and was at .243 for the season, with four home runs and 37 RBIs in 122 games.

Regular Yankees observers expected Dent to be lifted for a pinch-hitter. But that wasn't manager Bob Lemon's style. He had been brought in 10 weeks earlier to take over as manager of the Yankees after Billy Martin's tearful "resignation," and Lemon had taken his team this far by letting the players play and "staying out of the way." He wasn't going to change now.

Dent took Torrez's first pitch for a strike and then fouled the next pitch down on his foot and fell to the ground, writhing in pain. While trainer Gene Monahan sprinted to Dent's aid, spraying the injured area with ethyl chloride to deaden the pain, the on-deck batter, Mickey Rivers, had picked up Dent's bat and was examining it.

"Hey, homey," Rivers said. "You're using the wrong bat, man. That bat's cracked."

Rivers sent the batboy to the bat rack for another bat, which he handed to Dent.

"I didn't even think about it because my foot was hurting so much," Dent said. "I just took the bat and I went back up there, and the next pitch, he threw a fastball. He tried to get it in on me, but he got it down."

Said Torrez, "It really wasn't a bad pitch, but I didn't get it where I wanted to. What I was going to do was

Bucky Dent hits one of the most famous
home runs in Yankees history.

come in on him to knock him off the plate, and then come back with a slider away. It was going to be a wasted pitch, but it tailed back over the plate.

"When he hit it, I didn't think it was going out because I saw Yaz [Carl Yastrzemski] pop his glove, and anytime you see him pop his glove, the ball is catchable. So I said, 'Good, I'm out of the inning.'

"Then he kind of backed up, backed up, and then he hit the wall, and I'm going, 'Oh, shit,' and the ball went over the wall. Yaz dropped his head, and I said, 'Damn.'"

Said Dent, "When I hit the ball, I didn't know if it was high enough. I thought it was going to hit off the wall. I was the lead run, so I was trying to get to second base, running with my head down. When I rounded the bag at first, I saw the umpire signaling it was a home run.

"As I rounded second and third and was trotting toward home, Fenway was dead silent. You could hear a pin drop, except for the few Yankees fans. You could hear them clapping."

The Yankees had taken the lead, 3–2, but it still wasn't over. The Yankees tacked on another run in the seventh and one in the eighth to make it 5–2. And it still wasn't over. In this season of comebacks, the Red Sox had one more comeback left in them.

Weary from a long season, Guidry ran out of gas, and Goose Gossage had to come in to put down a Boston rally in the bottom of the seventh. But in the eighth, the Red Sox scored two runs and batted in the ninth, trailing 5–4.

In the ninth, the Red Sox put runners on first and second with one out and their two best hitters coming to bat: Jim Rice, who finished the season with a .315 average, a league-leading 46 homers, and 139 RBIs; and Yastrzemski, who had hit a home run earlier in the game.

Rice brought the Fenway Park crowd to their feet with a long drive to right field that Lou Piniella caught a few steps in front of the low-right-field fence.

Now it was Gossage against Yaz, a future Hall of Famer and Boston's biggest hero since Ted Williams. It was power against power, and Gossage didn't try anything fancy; he just fed Yastrzemski a diet of fastballs.

"That whole game was unbelievable," Gossage said. "I went to bed the night before thinking, 'Oh, man, I'll probably end up facing Yaz for the final out,' and, sure enough, there it was.

"I was so nervous and scared to death. My legs were banging together that if somebody had come out there to talk to me, I wouldn't even have known they were there. I was that nervous and that scared. I'd never come close to playing in a game of that magnitude."

Gossage reached back for something extra, and Yastrzemski took a healthy cut and hit a high, twisting pop-up toward third base that seemed like it took an eternity to come down.

Said Gossage, "[Graig] Nettles told me later that he was standing on third base, and when Yaz swung, he said to himself, 'Pop it up, pop it up, pop it up…' and when Yaz did pop it up, Nettles said, 'Oh, shit, not to me.'"

Dent: "Gossage threw a fastball right down the middle and Yastrzemski popped it up and Nettles caught the ball for the last out, and everybody rushed out of our dugout to jump on him. After the game, a friend said to me, 'Do you know what you just did?' I said, 'I hit a home run.' He said, 'No, it's going to change your life,' and he was right."

Manager Billy Martin congratulates Reggie Jackson on a job well done.

7. Reggie, Reggie, Reggie

The 1977 baseball season was like an interminable Greek tragedy played out in 162 acts, with epilogues and postscripts and curtain calls. It had failure and triumph, pathos and passion, heroes and villains. It had mysterious subplots and treachery, and, in the end, it had vindication and redemption.

For the Yankees, it began with the arrival at the team's spring training camp in Fort Lauderdale of Reggie Jackson, the game's premiere power hitter who had signed as a free agent. He came on the scene not with a whimper, but a flourish.

Upon his arrival, Jackson—who had said, "If I played in New York, they'd name a candy bar after me," and eventually they did—boasted, "I didn't come here to be a star; I brought my star with me."

From the start, his bravado irritated his new teammates, most especially his manager, Billy Martin, who made it clear he never wanted Jackson (he had implored the Yankees to sign Joe Rudi, Jackson's less flamboyant, but more well-rounded teammate, also a free agent).

As further evidence of his disdain for Jackson, Martin appeared to go out of his way to put Reggie in his place, embarrass him, and let him know who was boss. Martin batted Jackson sixth, instead of his customary and preferred fourth, and included his name on the travel list of every trip the Yankees made in Florida (stars generally were not asked to make every bus trip in spring training).

The Yankees won their season opener but then lost eight of their next nine games and fell into last place. However, they righted the ship, went on a six-game winning streak, and by mid-May had moved into first place. Then the magazine article hit.

Jackson had talked during spring training with a magazine writer and made his infamous statement: "I'm the straw that stirs the drink. [Thurman] Munson thinks he can be the straw that stirs the drink, but he can only stir it bad." The magazine came out on May 23.

Munson was stung by the words. The article caused a rift between him and Jackson that never completely healed. Munson's teammates, who respected their captain and viewed him as the heart and soul of the team, rallied around him. Martin sided with Munson. And Jackson, whose relations with his new teammates and his manager were already strained, became more of an outcast. If Jackson hit a home run, Munson, often batting in front of him, would not shake his hand.

By August 10, an uneasy peace had settled on the Yankees. Martin installed Jackson in the cleanup spot in the batting order and would keep him there for the remainder of the season. Jackson would hit 13 home runs and drive in 49 runs in the final 53 games, finishing with a .283 average, 32 homers, and 110 RBIs, to help carry the Yankees to their second straight American League East title, by two-and-a-half games over Boston and Baltimore.

For the second straight year, the Yankees faced the Kansas City Royals in the best-of-five American League Championship Series. They split the first four games, so it came down to Game 5 in Kansas City for the American League pennant, and once again controversy erupted in Yankeeland.

When he arrived at the ballpark, Jackson, to his chagrin, discovered he was not in the starting lineup for this crucial game.

"Billy slapping me down one more time," Jackson said.

Martin's rationale for his decision was that in the first four games, Jackson had only one hit in 14 at-bats and that the Royals' starter, Paul Splittorff, was the sort of left-hander that gave Jackson trouble.

Jackson got his chance in the eighth inning. With the Yankees trailing, 3–1, two men on, two outs, and Splittorff replaced by right-hander Doug Bird, Martin sent Jackson up as a pinch-hitter for Cliff Johnson. A home run would have given the Yankees a 4–3 lead, but Jackson's time for dramatic home runs had not yet come. He singled to make the score 3–2.

In the ninth, the Yankees scored three runs for a dramatic, come-from-behind 5–3 victory, and they were off to the World Series against the Los Angeles Dodgers.

"I'm the straw that stirs the drink. [Thurman] Munson thinks he can be the straw that stirs the drink, but he can only stir it bad."
—Reggie Jackson, quoted in *Sport* magazine shortly after he signed as a free agent with the Yankees in

---

Back in right field, and in the cleanup position, Jackson singled in the first game of the World Series, was hitless in four trips in the second game, and singled home a run in the third game as the Yankees won two of the first three games.

By Game 4, Jackson was in full form. He doubled leading off the second inning to jump-start a three-run rally and blasted a home run in the sixth in a 4–2 victory that gave the Yankees a three-games-to-one lead in the Series.

The Dodgers kept their hopes alive in Game 5. Jackson singled in the seventh and, in his final at-bat in the ninth, belted his second home run of the Series, a meaningless, window-dressing home run in a 10–4 game. But he was just warming up as the Yankees returned to Yankee Stadium needing one win in two games for their first World Series victory in 15 years.

October 18, 1977, was a cool, clear night in New York, a crowd of 56,407 gathering at Yankee Stadium for what they anticipated would be a coronation. Enthusiasm was stifled somewhat when the Dodgers scored twice in the first inning, but in the bottom of the second, Jackson led off with a walk and rode home on Chris Chambliss's game-tying home run.

Jackson batted for the second time in the fourth inning with the Dodgers ahead, 3–2, and Munson on first. He hit Burt Hooton's first pitch into the right-field seats to give the Yankees a 4–3 lead.

In the fifth, Jackson came up against reliever Elias Sosa with two outs and Willie Randolph on base. Again, Jackson crushed the first pitch into the right-field seats to boost the Yankees' lead to 7–3.

The issue was no longer in doubt when Jackson batted leading off the bottom of the eighth. This time the pitcher was knuckleballer Charlie Hough. Jackson was on center stage, the spotlight where he wanted it, beamed directly on him. He swung at the first pitch and drove it deep into the night, a monster shot into the center-field bleachers.

Three home runs on three pitches against three different pitchers! It was a hitting performance called by many the greatest in World Series history.

Going back to his last at-bat in Game 5, Jackson had hit home runs in four consecutive official at-bats on four consecutive pitches off four different pitchers. His three home runs in one game tied the World Series record set by Babe Ruth in 1926 and repeated by the Babe two years later. His five home runs set a World Series record. He would be dubbed "Mr. October" by, of all people, Thurman Munson.

As Jackson rounded the bases after his third homer in Game 6, the crowd chanted: "Reg-gie… Reg-gie…Reg-gie…."

Rounding third base and heading for home, Jackson blew kisses at the press level of the stadium, in the direction of the owner's box. When he reached the dugout, waiting for him there, ready to throw his arms around Jackson in a congratulatory embrace, was Billy Martin.

A Home of Their Own

In the first 10 years of their existence, the Yankees (they were the Highlanders in those days) played their home games at Hilltop Park on Broadway and 168th Street in upper Manhattan, the present site of Columbia Presbyterian Hospital. It was a rattletrap of a ballpark with 10,000 seats in wooden stands, and it was quickly becoming obsolete and a fire hazard.

Change was in the wind. It came in 1913, when the Highlanders became the Yankees and moved into a new home, the Polo Grounds, as tenants of the powerful and popular New York Giants of the National League, who had captured the fancy of New York fans of the new sport, baseball, by winning three pennants and one World Series in the first decade of the game's modern era.

It was an ideal arrangement for the Giants, collecting rent from the new team in town playing in the upstart American League–ideal as long as the Giants maintained their supremacy in the city.

But in 1920, along came Babe Ruth, with his booming, majestic home runs, and the pendulum began to swing. Although the Giants finished second in the National League and the Yankees third in the American League, the Yankees not only outdrew the Giants in their own home but also doubled their attendance of the previous year by attracting the unheard-of total of 1,289,422 fans–the first baseball team to attract more than 1 million fans at home in a season.

The rivalry between New York's two teams intensified when they met in the World Series of 1921 and 1922, all Series games played in one ballpark. It was no consolation to the Giants that they maintained their superiority over their new rival on the playing field by winning both Series. The indisputable fact was that the Yankees, because of the enormous popularity of Ruth, had emerged as the city's number-one team. Fans were switching their allegiance from the established Giants to the new team in town.

Something had to be done, and John McGraw, the Napoleonic leader/manager/part owner of the Giants did it. He informed the Yankees that their lease would not be renewed following the 1922 season.

With his team in danger of being homeless, Colonel Jacob Ruppert, who with Colonel Tillinghast L'Hommedieu had purchased the Yankees in 1915 for $460,000, moved swiftly. For $1.5 million he purchased 10 acres of swampland in the Bronx, across the Harlem River and a mile away from the Polo Grounds.

Construction began on a magnificent new structure on May 5, 1922. It took 45,000 cubic yards of earth as fill, 20,000 cubic yards of concrete, eight tons of reinforced steel, one million board feet of Pacific Coast fir for bleachers, and 284 days to build the edifice that would quickly become the most famous sports stadium in the world.

The state-of-the-art structure would be called Yankee Stadium and would come to be known as "the House that Ruth Built."

Wednesday, April 23, 1923, was a raw and windy day in New York City. The midday temperatures struggled vainly to climb into the 50s, but hearts and hides were warmed by the arrival of spring in New York, heralded by the opening of the baseball season.

On that day, Bloomingdale's announced a sale of men's two-trouser suits for $24.75. Loft's advertised chocolate-covered coconut candy for 24¢ a pound, and the A&P had Brer Rabbit molasses for 7¢, Grandmother's bread for 5¢, and Pacific toilet paper for 5¢ a roll.

Pola Negri was starring in *Bella Donna* at the Rivoli; Vera Sheppard completed a record 69 consecutive hours of dancing, and a raid on Oscar Carr's garage in Northampton uncovered a 250-gallon still and a large quantity of liquor and mash.

On April 18, 1923, the New York Yankees received a new home.

But the big news on that day was in the Bronx, where Governor Al Smith and Mayor John Hyland, baseball commissioner Kenesaw Mountain Landis, police commissioner Richard Enright, and bandmaster John Philip Sousa helped dedicate the newest, largest, most modern stadium in baseball.

There was no ballpark to be compared with the magnificent new edifice. Yankee Stadium was the last word in athletic facilities.

They came to the South Bronx by streetcar, by bus, by subway, and by automobile on that day, hordes of fans attracted by a sense of history, a feeling of pride, a spirit of togetherness. The official attendance was 74,217, with an additional 15,000 milling around outside, having been denied admittance to the stadium.

Those fortunate to make it inside had reason to be uplifted—by the beautiful surroundings, by watching Yankees shortstop Everett Scott play in his 986th consecutive game, by Bob Shawkey's three-hitter against the Boston Red Sox. But the highlight of the day came early, in the third inning, when, fittingly, Ruth hit the first home run in the new stadium, a "four-base drive into the right-field bleachers with two mates on that drove the fans into a frenzy," according to the *New York Daily News*.

In time, Yankee Stadium became the best-known sports palace in the world.

It was there that Knute Rockne of Notre Dame made his famous "win one for the Gipper" speech in 1928 and Army battled heavily favored Notre Dame to a scoreless tie in 1948.

It was there that Joe Louis knocked out Max Schmeling, the pride of Nazi Germany, in the first round in 1938, and Sugar Ray Robinson melted under June heat and humidity against light heavyweight champion Joey Maxim in 1952.

It was there that Roger Maris hit his 61st home run in 1961, and Don Larsen pitched the only perfect game in World Series history in 1956.

It was there that thousands bade weepy farewells to Lou Gehrig and Babe Ruth.

Yankee Stadium has been the scene of more World Series than any other stadium. It has housed three NFL championship games, 30 title fights, 19 Fordham-NYU and 21 Army–Notre Dame football games.

Pope Paul VI, Pope John II, and Pope John Paul II celebrated mass there, Billy Graham and Billy Sunday preached there, Nelson Mandela was greeted there, George W. Bush threw out the first ball there, Billy Joel, U2, Pink Floyd, and the Beach Boys performed there.

The Bronx became baseball's capital, Yankee Stadium its castle, and Babe Ruth its sultan.

If Yankee Stadium wasn't actually "the House that Ruth Built," it was the house that Ruth made legendary.

In 1976 Chris Chambliss helped give the Yankees their first pennant since 1964.

9 Chambliss Touches Them All

It had been 12 years since the Yankees' last pennant, their longest championship drought since they won their first one all the way back in 1921.

Now, on the night of October 14, 1976, they were one win away from once again ascending to the top of the American League.

It had been a season of revival for the Yankees, with a new manager (Billy Martin was in his first full season as bench leader), a new owner with a hunger to win and the willingness to spend whatever it took to do so (George Steinbrenner, in his fourth year as boss of the Yankees, pushed for trades that brought Mickey Rivers, Willie Randolph, Oscar Gamble, Ed Figueroa, Carlos May, Ken Holtzman, Doyle Alexander, and Grant Jackson to New York), and a remodeled ballpark (Yankee Stadium had been closed for two years for renovations, at a cost of $100 million, reopening on April 15 of that year).

The Yankees won the American League East by a healthy 10½ games and met the Kansas City Royals in the best-of-five American League Championship Series. The two teams split the first four games, and it all came down to this one game for the pennant, with 56,821 hopeful but nervous fans as witnesses in the renovated stadium.

John Mayberry gave the Royals an early lead with a two-run homer off Figueroa in the first, but the Yankees came right back with two runs in the bottom of the first, two in the third, and two more in the sixth.

Yankee Stadium was abuzz with anticipation as the Royals batted in the top of the eighth. The joy turned to gloom when George Brett, who had plagued the Yankees throughout his career, exploded a dramatic, clutch three-run blast that tied the score, 6–6, and shocked the capacity crowd into an eerie silence.

The tension heightened when the Yankees failed to score in the bottom of the eighth, and Dick Tidrow came in to shut down the Royals in the top of the ninth.

The Yankees went to the bottom of the ninth with first baseman Chris Chambliss due to lead off against right-hander Mark Littell, who had shut the Yankees down since the seventh inning.

Chambliss had come to the Yankees along with Tidrow from Cleveland two years before in a controversial trade for four pitchers. Chambliss solidified the Yankees' first-base position and came to be admired as a quiet leader, humble, unassuming, and dependable. During the season, he had batted .293, hit 17 home runs, and driven in 96 runs. In this ALCS, he was batting .500, 10 hits in 20 at-bats, including a two-run homer in Game 3.

Now fate had him in the center of baseball's biggest stage.

"There was a long delay before I got up to hit," Chambliss remembered. "People were throwing paper and stuff on the field, and the groundskeepers had to clear the field, so I had a long wait before I stepped up to the plate. It was cold and I was waiting, and it was kind of an anxious moment."

"You don't even know how to spell IQ." —Oscar Gamble, during a debate with teammate Carlos May over which player had the higher IQ

Once he finally got into the batter's box, Chambliss didn't have to wait long. He jumped all over Littell's first pitch and sent it soaring high and far into the night, headed for the right-field seats.

"Al Cowens, the right fielder, went back like he had a bead on it," said Chambliss, "but right at the end, he put his head against the wall and the ball went over. I didn't know it was going out until it got out there. It wasn't one of those no-doubters, you know, when you hit it you know it's gone. This one just cleared the fence, but I knew it had a chance when I hit it."

The ball disappeared into the seats, and Yankee Stadium erupted. Bedlam! Fans, mingling with jubilant Yankees players, poured onto the field. They swarmed all over the place, collecting souvenirs. They pulled up chunks of sod, grabbed for players' caps, ripped bases out of the ground in a celebration gone amok.

"Running around the bases, I remember touching first and second," said Chambliss. "And then somebody tripped me between short and third. I got up and people were trying to steal my helmet, so I took my helmet off and put it under my arm like a football. Third base was ridiculous. There were people all over the place, and the base had to have been stolen by then. I went around them and went close to the other team's dugout, then I just took a beeline to our dugout because home plate was also full of people.

"There was a guy in front of our dugout, and I just walked right over him. I gave him a little shoulder block to get into that dugout."

Fans streamed out of their seats and swarmed all over the field as the Yankees dashed for the cover of their clubhouse. Inside, they shouted and pounded one another on the back and embraced in victory, popping open bottles of champagne to spray the room, and each other, with the bubbly.

Somebody asked Chambliss if he touched every base. He said he thought so, but wasn't sure. It was suggested that he go back on the field and do it again, just for good measure, and he did.

Minutes later, with fans still swarming around the infield, with the Royals already in their clubhouse, Chambliss returned to the field with a police escort and went to third base and stomped the ground where he figured third base had been. He then went to where home plate had been and did the same thing. He made sure to touch every base. He touched them all, and the Yankees had reached the World Series for the first time in 12 years.

Requiem for a Streak

Baseball players aren't always the last to know, at least not all players. Lou Gehrig knew before anyone else. It was time to sit, to put an end to his amazing iron-man streak. He had played in a remarkable 2,130 consecutive games that spanned 15 seasons, but Gehrig knew it was over.

In those 15 seasons, he would bat over .300 13 times, with a high of .379 in 1930, drive in more than 100 runs for 13 straight years, including an American League record 184 in 1931, and hit 493 home runs. And he would not miss a game, playing despite broken bones and pulled muscles.

The first inkling that it was over came to Gehrig in the 1938 season, small, subtle signs: a 56-point decline in his batting average of the previous year, from .351 to .295; his home runs down from 37 to 29; RBIs down from 138 to 115. Nothing alarming there. Gehrig was past his 35th birthday, an age when production normally declines.

But those who knew him best suspected there was some problem other than age. Gehrig never complained about anything physical–he was, after all, the indestructible man, the "Iron Horse"–but his frustration at a loss of power manifested itself in an uncharacteristic number of thrown bats.

"To see that big guy coming back to the dugout after striking out with the bases loaded would make your heart bleed," said teammate Lefty Gomez.

In the 1938 World Series against the Cubs, Gehrig had managed only four hits, all singles, in 14 at-bats–no runs batted in from a player who had batted .371, smacked 10 home runs, and driven in 35 runs in six previous World Series. No reason for panic there, either. Just a little slump. Any player can have a little slump, this one just happened to come at an inopportune time.

Gehrig shrugged off his season decline and World Series failure, accepted a $3,000 pay cut that lowered his salary to $36,000, and reported to spring training in 1939 determined to work harder than ever to restore his numbers to their customary lofty status.

But by mid-March, Gehrig had played in only 10 exhibition games, his average was barely over .100, and he had failed to get an extra-base hit. His reflexes had slowed, his once enormous power was almost nonexistent, and he labored doing even the simplest things on the field that once he had performed so instinctively.

Again, Gehrig dismissed the signs. He was aging, and this was only spring training. He would get it all going again once the season started, the games had meaning, and the adrenaline had started flowing.

But the adrenaline didn't flow; things did not change. On May 2, the Yankees went to Detroit to open a series against the Tigers. They had played eight games, and Gehrig was batting .143. He had been to bat 28 times and had just four hits, all singles, and one RBI.

Upon the team's arrival in Detroit, Gehrig sought out manager Joe McCarthy in the hotel lobby. He told McCarthy he needed to talk with him. McCarthy invited Gehrig to the manager's room.

"I'm benching myself, Joe," Gehrig said.

"Why?" the manager asked.

"For the good of the team, Joe," Gehrig said. "Nobody has to tell me how bad I've been and how much of a drawback I've been to the club. I've been thinking ever since the season opened, when I couldn't start as I hoped I would, that the time has come for me to quit."

Such a decision could only come from Gehrig himself. McCarthy would have let him go on, let him continue the streak as long as he wanted to play. But Gehrig was too proud to accept a free pass when he was hurting the team.

Lou Gehrig (shown here with his arm around Ellsworth "Babe" Dahlgren) played in 2,130 consecutive games before finally taking himself out of the lineup.

That afternoon, as captain of the Yankees, Gehrig carried the lineup card to home plate, a lineup that for the first time in 14 years did not include his name. And then Gehrig returned to the dugout and fought back tears as an announcement was made that he would not be in the starting lineup. The Detroit crowd gave Gehrig a standing ovation, and then Lou took a seat on the bench and watched Babe Dahlgren take his place at first base.

The streak had started on June 1, 1925, when Gehrig appeared as a pinch-hitter. The next day, he played first base in place of veteran Wally Pipp, who had been hit on the head with a pitch in batting practice. Pipp was sold to Cincinnati the following winter, and Gehrig went on to play in 2,130 consecutive games.

Now, exactly one month short of 14 years after he replaced Pipp at first base, the Iron Man's streak was over. Lou Gehrig would never play another game for the Yankees.

Mickey Mantle goes to bat in spite of the pain.

Mantle Blasts Off

The Mickey Mantle legend began in his first spring training, in 1951, when, as a 19-year-old rookie he startled and excited veteran baseball observers with his awesome power by hitting prodigious home runs to faraway places. It didn't matter that many of his monster shots were given impetus by the rarefied air of Arizona. The legend was born.

Mantle first caught the Yankees' attention in his second professional season. Playing in Joplin as an 18-year-old shortstop, he batted a robust .383, showed his speed with 12 triples, and unveiled his power with 26 home runs and 136 RBIs in 137 games, which earned him an invitation to spring training.

Veteran sportswriters, happy to have someone new as a subject for their stories, were captivated by the youngster who was part Greek god and part cartoon character: a blond Adonis with bulging muscles and a wonderful, alliterative name. Awed by his power and speed, they dubbed him the Commerce Comet (Mantle was born in Spavinaw, Oklahoma, but was raised in Commerce).

Even his new teammates were impressed, and amused, by the country boy from Oklahoma.

"He was a funny-looking guy," remembered Billy Martin. "He wore jeans and plaid shirts most of the time, and his hair was cut short. It looked like it had been chopped up with a penknife. He had these big forearms like Li'l Abner. In fact, he sounded like Li'l Abner when he talked.

"When he got in the batting cage, I couldn't believe my eyes. His power was tremendous. I watched him hit a couple in the seats right-handed and then turn around and hit a couple more in the seats left-handed, and I'm thinking, 'Who's that show-off?'"

The writers were sending stories back to their papers about the new kid, and, through those stories, we learned that Mickey was his real name, not a nickname.

That was the name on his birth certificate. His father had named him after his favorite ballplayer, Mickey Cochrane, the Hall of Fame catcher of the Detroit Tigers.

We also learned that Mantle's father, who worked in the Oklahoma zinc mines, was a passionate baseball fan who had the foresight to make his son a switch-hitter and that Mantle had been signed for the Yankees by a scout named Tom Greenwade; and we added a new word to our vocabulary: *osteomyelitis*, the bone disease that had afflicted Mantle as a teenager and would plague him throughout his career.

The Yankees brought Mantle with them to New York to open the 1951 season, but he struck out too often and was sent down to Kansas City, the Yankees' Triple A affiliate in the American Association. After a few months, Mantle returned to the Yankees to play right field alongside the great Joe DiMaggio. It was while playing right field in the 1951 World Series against the Giants that Mantle stepped in a drainage ditch chasing a fly ball hit by Willie Mays and tore up his knee, sidelining him for the remainder of the Series and setting in motion a seemingly endless string of leg injuries.

In 1952 DiMaggio had retired, and Mantle took over center field for the Yankees, where he would remain for 15 spectacular years. The Yankees learned to live with his strikeouts because when he made contact, he hit balls to places few others could reach.

The Mantle legend grew in 1953 with a home run hit right-handed that went clear out of Washington's Griffith Stadium and was measured at 562 feet, and the legend reached its zenith on the night of May 22, 1963.

Many in the sparse crowd of 10,312 had left Yankee Stadium when Mantle came to bat leading off the bottom of the eleventh inning of a 7–7 tie. Batting left-handed against

Bill Fischer of the Kansas City Royals, Mantle put a charge into a 2–2 pitch and drove it high and far toward the upper deck in right field.

The ball was a rocket soaring high toward the stadium's famous façade, which measured 108 feet and one inch high in old Yankee Stadium before its renovation. Mantle's drive banged off the façade, only inches from going clear out of the famous old stadium.

Mantle called it "the hardest ball I ever hit."

Coach Frank Crosetti, who played with Babe Ruth and Lou Gehrig, went further. "That's the hardest I've ever seen anyone hit a ball. Foxx, Ruth, anybody. I don't believe anyone can hit a ball any harder. It went out like it was shot out of a cannon."

The shot was measured at 535 feet (he hit three others that were longer) and was the 413th of his 536 home runs.

It might have been symbolic that only six days before the Yankees' No. 7 sent a baseball into orbit in Yankee Stadium, astronaut Gordon Cooper, piloting the spaceship *Faith 7*, had completed a 22-orbit mission around the moon.

For years triviots had been asking the question, "Has a fair ball ever been hit out of Yankee Stadium?"

The answer always was "no."

But on the night of May 22, 1963, Mickey Mantle came inches away from having that question answered in the affirmative.

12. A Brave New World

One way to measure the unparalleled success of the Yankees is through the tenures of their managers.

Miller Huggins won six pennants and three World Series, Joe McCarthy eight pennants and seven World Series, Casey Stengel 10 pennants and seven World Series, Ralph Houk three pennants and two World Series, and Billy Martin two pennants and one World Series. Joe Torre is in place to outdo them all.

Each manager has had his defining moment, and Torre's came in Atlanta on October 23, 1996, Game 4 of the World Series against the Braves.

When the Yankees sought a successor to Buck Showalter as manager after the 1995 season, Torre was a compromise choice, depicted as "Clueless Joe" in one New York tabloid because of a spotty record in three previous managerial stints. In 14 seasons as field boss of the Mets, Braves, and Cardinals, he had finished higher than fourth just seven times, had made the postseason once, and had an overall record of 986–1,073.

But in his first year with the Yankees, Torre guided them to 92 wins and the American League East title by four games over Baltimore. They then beat Texas, three games to one, in the division series, and the Orioles, four games to one, in the American League Championship Series to win the 34th pennant in the team's history and advance to the World Series for the first time in 15 years.

The Yankees' World Series opponents, the Braves, defending Series champs, had won their sixth consecutive National League East title. They did it with baseball's most dominant pitching staff headed by John Smoltz, Greg Maddux, and Tom Glavine, and went into the World Series as clear-cut favorites to repeat as champions.

When they won the first two games of the Series at Yankee Stadium, a 12–1 rout in Game 1 behind Smoltz,

and a 4–0 shutout in Game 2 behind Maddux, it seemed inevitable that the Braves would finish off the Yankees at home, avoid a return trip to New York, and win their second straight World Series.

Torre believed otherwise. He boldly told a worried and nervous team owner, George Steinbrenner, "Don't worry, boss, we'll beat them four straight."

Was Torre prescient? Was it merely wishful thinking? Or was he simply trying to get Steinbrenner off his back? It was likely that should he lose the World Series, Torre would find himself out of a job once more.

The tomahawk-choppers were out in force for Game 3 in Atlanta on October 22, but the Yankees muted the premature celebration with a 5–2 victory as David Cone outdueled Glavine. Bernie Williams put the game away with a two-run homer in a three-run eighth, and John Wetteland pitched a perfect ninth for the save.

For Game 4, Atlanta fans put on a brave front. Their Braves were still in command of the Series, and they had their aces, Smoltz and Maddux, in reserve for Games 5 and 6. The revelry at Turner Field reached a crescendo when the Braves bombed Kenny Rogers for five runs in the first three innings, added another run in the fourth, and took a 6–0 lead into the sixth inning of the fourth game.

Six runs down and with only 12 outs remaining, the Yankees awoke. Looking for omens, one might point to Derek Jeter's foul pop leading off the top of the sixth, a ball that should have been caught and, under normal circumstances, would have been caught. But umpire Tim Welke interfered with Braves right fielder Jermaine Dye, and the ball dropped untouched, giving Jeter, and the Yankees, life.

Jeter took advantage of his good fortune by hitting a single to right, opening the door for a three-run rally that cut the Braves' lead in half and gave the Yankees hope.

Jeff Nelson, Mariano Rivera, and Graeme Lloyd held the Braves in check into the eighth inning, when the Yankees came to bat still trailing, 6–3, and quickly running out of time.

To start the eighth, Atlanta manager Bobby Cox called on his closer, Mark Wohlers, he of the 100-mile-per-hour fastball. Wohlers had compiled 39 saves during the regular season and five more in six appearances in the division and League Championship Series, without allowing a run. He had pitched an inning against the Yankees in Game 2, faced four men, and struck out three of them.

"We play today; we win today."
—Mariano Duncan, during the Yankees run to a pennant in 1996

Braves fans were confident Wohlers would hold off the Yankees and close out the victory, but there was more bad karma in the eighth. Charlie Hayes led off with a nubber down the third-base line that Chipper Jones let roll, expecting it to go foul. The ball hugged the line and came to rest in fair territory as Hayes reached first. Darryl Strawberry followed with a single, but Mariano Duncan hit a ground ball to short, a perfect double-play ball. Rafael Belliard, installed for defense in the seventh, bobbled the ball long enough for Duncan to beat the relay throw to first and avoid the double play.

That brought up Jim Leyritz, who had gone in to catch after Joe Girardi was lifted for a pinch-hitter in the sixth. With no extra catchers on his bench, Torre was forced to stay with Leyritz, who had batted .264 in 88 regular-season games with seven home runs and 40 RBIs. In the Series, he had just one single in four at-bats.

Pumping nothing but 100-mile-per-hour fastballs, as he had done the entire inning, Wohlers ran the count to 2–2 on Leyritz. Here the pitcher made a tactical error. Instead of firing another fastball, his best pitch, he tried to fool Leyritz with a slider. Not only was it Wohlers's second-best pitch, a no-no in such a critical situation, it served to speed up Leyritz's bat. The slider came in flat, and Leyritz tattooed it over the outstretched glove of left fielder Andruw Jones into the seats for a dramatic, game-tying, three-run homer.

The Yankees had come all the way back from a six-run deficit, and they would not be denied. After two were out in the top of the tenth, they rallied for two runs and an 8–6 victory that tied the Series at two games apiece.

There still was work to be done, and the Yankees did it, as Andy Pettitte beat Smoltz, 1–0, in Game 5. In Game 6, the Yankees scored three in the third off Maddux and held on for a 3–2 victory to win their first World Series in 18 years, just as Torre had promised.

There were several Yankees heroes, including Wetteland, who saved all four World Series victories, and Williams, who drove in four runs, but none bigger than Leyritz. His three-run, game-tying home run in Game 4 turned the Series around and set the tone for the Yankees to win four world championships in the first five years of Joe Torre's managerial reign.

Babe Ruth becomes the home-run king.

Going Like 60

When Babe Ruth raised his own single-season home-run record to 59 in 1921, his second season with the Yankees, observers wondered how high was up. Would the mighty Babe raise the bar to 60 homers? To 70? Higher?

The year after Ruth's record haul, Commissioner Kenesaw Mountain Landis suspended the Babe for the first month of the season for participating in an unauthorized barnstorming tour. He hit only 35 home runs in 1922.

In the next two seasons, Ruth returned to his customary place as home-run king. He led the league in 1923 with 41 homers and in 1924 with 46 and celebrated by going off to Cuba for a vacation of revelry. He partied, drank, ate, and reportedly blew his entire 1924 salary at the gaming tables.

When he reported for spring training in 1925, Ruth was 30 pounds overweight. His complexion was sallow, and he looked haggard, drawn, and run-down despite the added weight. His face was puffy, his eyes sunken and bloodshot.

"Everybody figured he was washed up," said teammate Earle Combs. "He was just a wreck."

At the start of spring training, Ruth came down with the flu. Then he broke a finger in a clubhouse prank. When he had recovered, he worked hard to lose the excess weight, but he also continued to party hard. On the trip north, the Yankees stopped off to play a game in Asheville, North Carolina. As the Babe climbed off the Pullman, his face turned gray, he started gasping for breath, his eyes closed, and he tottered and then pitched face first onto the cement platform.

Ruth was rushed to a local hospital, and the New York newspapers, in blaring headlines, intimated the mighty Bambino was at death's door. He was transferred to a New York hospital for tests, and the official word was that Ruth was suffering from influenza and indigestion—one writer referred to it as "the stomach ache heard 'round the world," but most suspected they were not being told the true nature of Babe's ailment. Rumors abounded that Ruth had been stricken by a social disease.

Ruth remained hospitalized while the Yankees lost 16 of their first 24 games. By the last week of May, Ruth checked himself out of the hospital and began working out. Against the advice of his doctors, he returned to the lineup on June 1, still in a weakened condition. That didn't stop him from continuing his reckless lifestyle.

On an August trip to St. Louis, the Babe vanished once the team hit town and did not show up until five minutes before game time the following day. Manager Miller Huggins fined him $5,000 and suspended him indefinitely, causing Ruth to blow his top.

"I ought to choke you to death," Ruth threatened his manager.

To the press, Ruth said, "I will not play for him. Either he quits or I quit."

General manager Ed Barrow interceded and struck a truce between Ruth and Huggins. Ruth's suspension was lifted after nine days, and he returned to the lineup on September 9, but he finished the season with a mere 25 home runs in 98 games.

Back on track the following year, Ruth again led the American League in home runs with 47, but by the start of spring training, 1927, it appeared the Babe's best home-run-hitting days were behind him. He was 32 years old, and he had not hit more than 47 homers in five years. His 59 home runs in 1921 were viewed as the ultimate, a record that would never be broken.

In the 1927 season, the Yankees exploded out of the starting gate like a runaway train. On July 5, they swept the Washington Senators in a doubleheader, 12–1 and 21–1, and opened a 12-game lead in the American League.

The *New York World* had retained Ruth to contribute a weekly column, and in it, he wrote: "If I am to break my 1921 record, I believe I will do it this year.... There is one thing that makes me think I can better the 59 mark, and that's Lou Gehrig. Having him follow me in the batting order has helped me a lot."

In the first week of July, Gehrig had 28 home runs, two more than Ruth. By late August, Gehrig faded in the home-run race, while Ruth carried on. He entered the month of September with 43 blasts and continued his assault.

On September 29, Babe hit two home runs against the Senators, numbers 58 and 59, matching his 1921 record. There were still two games remaining in the season.

On September 30, Ruth came to bat in the eighth inning against Washington's Tom Zachary. The score was tied, 2–2, and Ruth tore into a pitch with a crack that, according to one newspaper account, "was audible in all parts of the stands. It was not necessary to follow the course of the ball. The boys in the bleachers indicated the route of the record homer."

The ball landed in the upper deck at Yankee Stadium, just inside the right-field foul pole, although for years Zachary insisted that the ball was foul.

Despite Zachary's contention, home run number 60 went into the record books.

Ruth's 60 home runs were 13 more than Gehrig, the American League runner-up, 42 more than the number three man, Tony Lazzeri, and exactly twice as many as the National League co-leaders, Hack Wilson and Cy Williams. It also was more home runs than were hit by any other American League team and by 12 of the 16 teams in the major leagues.

Babe Ruth had done the impossible and reached the unreachable: He had hit 60 home runs in a season and established a record that everyone agreed would never be equaled.

Jeter Flips

Where did he come from?

Why was he there?

Call it instinct, anticipation, the ability to be in the right place at the right time and to do the little things that win games, qualities that have made Derek Jeter a special player throughout his decade with the Yankees.

He had come to the Yankees at the age of 21 for 15 games late in the 1995 season after four years up the ladder of their farm system, a first-round pick, sixth overall, in the June 1992 free-agent draft. He was the hope of the future. The following season, under a new manager, Joe Torre, Jeter was the Opening Day shortstop, a huge responsibility for one so young on a team with championship ambitions.

It soon became obvious that Jeter was a rookie in name only. He didn't play like a rookie. He didn't carry himself like a rookie. He had poise and baseball savvy and leadership qualities beyond his years and outside the realm of his brief experience.

In his first season, he batted .314, had 183 hits, scored 104 runs, drove in 78, and gave the Yankees solid defense at the critical shortstop position. Most important, he helped the Yankees win their first World Series in 18 years.

Over the next few years, Jeter improved and grew to become regarded as one of the premiere shortstops in the game and by the Yankees as their on-field leader. He pounded out more than 200 hits for three straight years, scored more than 100 runs for six straight years, led the league in runs scored in 1998 and in hits in 1999.

By 2001, Jeter was a full-fledged star, the Yankees' heart and soul, and their captain, a position held previously by such all-time Yankees greats as Lou Gehrig, Thurman Munson, and Don Mattingly. When the Yankees needed a clutch hit, Jeter was there to get it. When they needed a big play in the field, Jeter was there to make it.

Now, in the third game of the 2001 American League Division Series against the Oakland Athletics, with the Yankees trailing two games to none in the best-of-five series and playing in Oakland's Network Associates Coliseum, the Yankees needed a big play, and Jeter gave it to them.

It was not a spectacular catch with the tying run on base, or a far-ranging, back-handed stab of a ball in the hole and a long throw to first to nip the runner as the winning run was racing for home. It was not something that shows up in the box score. But instinct, quick thinking, and remarkable baseball savvy enabled Jeter to make the play that allowed the Yankees to go on to win their 38th American League pennant.

It came in the seventh inning with the Yankees clinging to a one-run lead. They had lost the first two games of the series at Yankee Stadium, their bats held in check by Mark Mulder and Tim Hudson, two of Oakland's young guns. No team had ever lost the first two games at home and come back to win a best-of-five series, and now the Yankees were forced to win the next two games in Oakland, where the A's had won 17 straight games.

The Yankees had scored a run in the fifth off Oakland's third young gun, Barry Zito, on a home run by Jorge Posada, and Mike Mussina nursed that slim lead into the seventh, when the A's staged a two-out rally. Jason Giambi's younger, less-famous, less-gifted brother, Jeremy, rifled a single to right, and Terrence Long followed with a drive into the right-field corner.

Right fielder Shane Spencer ran the ball down and aimlessly fired it back toward the infield. It sailed over the head of the cutoff man, second baseman Alfonso Soriano. It sailed over the head of first baseman Tino Martinez, backing up Soriano. It was headed for no-man's-land, the

Derek Jeter proves himself to be invaluable on the field.

unprotected area between first base and home plate, as Giambi chugged around the bases, certain to score the tying run without a play; certain, too, to send the Athletics on their way to a three-game sweep of the defending world champion Yankees.

Out of nowhere, all the way from his shortstop position, came Jeter to grab the errant throw and, in one motion, flip it like a tennis player's backhand to catcher Posada, who put the tag on a startled Giambi.

Why was Jeter there?

"It was my job to read the play," Jeter would later explain.

How many other shortstops would have been there? The Yankees don't practice that play. No team does.

Rescued by Jeter's quick reaction, the Yankees would win the game, 1–0, with Mariano Rivera pitching two scoreless innings for the save. They would win the next day and then return to Yankee Stadium to take Game 5 and the series. And they would beat the Seattle Mariners, four games to one, in the American League Championship Series to advance to the World Series for the fifth time in Jeter's six years as their shortstop.

It would not have happened, none of it, if Derek Jeter did not have the instincts, the anticipation, and the savvy to be in the right place at the right time.

Yankees owners Tillinghast Huston and Jacob Ruppert stand to the left of Babe Ruth and New York Governor Nathan Miller in 1921.

First of Many

The natives were getting restless, none more than the owner of the team. He wanted a championship, and he wanted it now.

In the seven years Colonel Jacob Ruppert owned the Yankees, the team had shown improvement on the field and at the box office. No longer were they second-class citizens to the Giants in New York City. No longer were they the town's baseball stepchildren. In fact, they had become number one in New York, the more popular team. They even outdrew the Giants in their own stadium, the Polo Grounds.

But they had not won a championship, and Ruppert, the beer baron who had everything, was getting restless.

It had been 18 years since New York's American League team had moved from Baltimore, and not only had they not won a pennant, they were perennial tail-enders, finishing in the second division (fifth or lower in an eight-team league) nine times. Not even the arrival of Miller Huggins as manager two years earlier, or Babe Ruth, the game's greatest slugger, could put the Yankees over the top.

In 1920, Ruth's first year in New York, the Yankees became the first New York team to attract more than 1 million paying customers to their home games, a fact that rankled the Giants and their manager and co-owner, John McGraw. Yet despite Ruth's lethal bat that produced 54 home runs and 137 runs batted in, the Yankees finished in third place in the American League for the second straight year.

And third place was not good enough for the colonel.

In an effort to remedy the situation, Jacob Ruppert hired Ed Barrow away from the Red Sox. Barrow had become manager of the Red Sox in 1918 and led them to victory in the World Series (the last Series the Sox would win for 86 years). Ruppert offered Barrow the job of general manager of the Yankees for the sole purpose of building a championship team, a move that raised suspicions in baseball circles. Was this the trailer to the sale of Ruth to the Yankees?

On the contrary, Barrow had been vehemently opposed to the sale of Ruth. It was Barrow who had recognized Ruth's bat as a weapon unmatched in the game and his greater value as an everyday player than as a pitcher. In 1917, the year before Barrow arrived in Boston, Ruth had been used exclusively as a pitcher, winning 24 games. When Barrow took over as manager, he split Ruth's time between pitching and playing the outfield. By 1919, the Babe was a full-time outfielder and part-time pitcher for the Red Sox.

One of Barrow's first moves as general manager of the Yankees was to engineer a deal with the Red Sox that brought catcher Wally Schang and pitcher Waite Hoyt to New York. Schang became the Yankees' regular catcher in 1921, batting .316 with six home runs and 55 RBIs. Hoyt won 19 games and augmented a pitching staff that included 27-game winner Carl Mays and 18-game winner Bob Shawkey.

Ruth had what many consider his greatest year, a .378 batting average, a record 59 home runs, and a league-leading 177 RBIs.

The Yankees battled the Indians down to the wire in the American League and clinched the pennant on the next-to-last day of the season by sweeping a doubleheader from the Philadelphia Athletics, 5–3 and 7–6, in 11 innings. Surprisingly, Ruth's bat was not a factor in the clinching sweep. He was hitless in the first game and had just one hit in the second game. One newspaper said of Ruth's performance that day, "He couldn't hit a box car with a handful of shot."

If Ruth's bat was silent in the clincher, he made a major contribution nonetheless in what was once a familiar role for him. He was brought in to pitch the eleventh inning of the second game of the doubleheader (he had started one other game earlier in the season) and was the winning pitcher in relief in the game in which the Yankees clinched their first pennant.

The 1921 World Series was the first Subway Series. To be precise, no subway was required, as all games were played in one ballpark, the Polo Grounds, with the landlord Giants prevailing over their tenants, five games to three.

The outcome of the World Series was not a satisfactory one for Ruppert. The joy of winning a pennant was short-lived and diminished by losing in the World Series, especially to the other team in town. It was not enough for him to merely get to the World Series; his goal was to win it.

But at least this was a start.

Once they got the hang of it, the Yankees continued to win pennants. In the 44-year period from 1921 to 1964, they would win 29 pennants, or 66 percent of the American League flags. Never again would they have an 18-year championship drought.

16. The Shipbuilder

"We plan on absentee ownership...I'll stick to building ships and let the baseball people run the team."

The words, in light of subsequent events over more than three decades, have been thrown back at him many times, but there was no hint on the afternoon of January 3, 1973, of what lay ahead.

George M. Steinbrenner III of Lorain, Ohio, was introduced as managing general partner and the head of a 12-man group that had purchased the Yankees from the Columbia Broadcasting System. The purchase price was $10 million in cash, $3.2 million less than CBS had paid for the team nine years before and $5 million less than its intrinsic value as calculated by National Economics Research Associates. Today, the value of the Yankees is estimated at somewhere between $700 million and $1 billion.

After eight years of ownership, during which the Yankees finished above fifth place just once and their home attendance fell below 1 million for the first time in 27 years, CBS decided it was not suited for the baseball business. The network was losing money. It was, basically, an absentee owner. And it had people running the Yankees who had no previous experience in baseball. Its board of directors handed down orders to find a buyer for the team.

The search led to Cleveland and Steinbrenner.

Who was this man, George M. Steinbrenner III? As a boy and a young man, he had starred as a multi-sport athlete at Culver Military Academy and at Williams College. Later, he would serve as an assistant football coach at Northwestern and Purdue, believing his calling was that he become a football coach.

His first fling at sports ownership was with the Cleveland Pipers of the American Basketball League, where he hired John McLendon to become the first black person to be a head coach in a major sports league.

At the behest of his father, Steinbrenner entered the family business, Kinsman Marine, which carried iron ore, coal, and grain on the Great Lakes. He built it into the American Shipbuilding Company, and in a short time tripled its revenues with $200 million in annual sales. In 1970, *Fortune* magazine named Steinbrenner, age 40, one of the nation's 12 Movers and Shakers.

But in New York, he was unknown.

It was through Gabe Paul, the longtime baseball executive then serving as president and general manager of the Cleveland Indians, that Steinbrenner learned that CBS was looking to sell the Yankees. Recognizing it as an opportunity of a lifetime, Steinbrenner put together a group of businessmen, most of them from Cleveland, and headed up a limited partnership that bought the team.

"We plan on absentee ownership. We're not going to pretend we're something we aren't. I'll stick to building ships...I won't be active in the day-to-day operation of the club at all." —George M. Steinbrenner, on January 3, 1973, at the time it was announced that he was heading a group that would purchase the Yankees from CBS

"It's the best buy in sports today," Steinbrenner said on the day the sale was announced. "I think it's a bargain. This is a dream come true. The Yankees are the greatest name in sports. Owning the Yankees is like owning the *Mona Lisa*."

"Owning the Yankees is like owning the *Mona Lisa*." —George Steinbrenner, after purchasing the team from CBS

In 1973, George Steinbrenner (right) became the Yankees' owner and became more hands-on than he ever imagined he would be. At left is Michael Burke, president of the Yankees under CBS ownership.

To close observers of the Yankees scene, it might have been viewed as a sign of things to come when Steinbrenner showed up in Fort Lauderdale for his first spring training as the team's owner and made notes, which he turned over to manager Ralph Houk and general manager Lee MacPhail, singling out players in need of a hair cut or those who looked disheveled in uniform.

"That player, No. 37," Steinbrenner charged, "has his hat on backwards."

"He's a catcher, George," he was told. "He's supposed to wear his hat backwards."

Steinbrenner began to spend more time with the Yankees, even showing up for a series in Texas, much to the dismay of Houk and the players. Gene Michael, the Yankees' shortstop in the first year of Steinbrenner's reign and one of the team's more fun-loving players, recalled one particular incident involving Steinbrenner's penchant for being an involved owner. Michael was known for an aversion to insects and other objects that crawl, as well as slime, phobias often exploited by his teammates.

"We were playing the Rangers in Texas and Steinbrenner was there, sitting in a box seat next to our dugout," Michael said. "While we were at bat, somebody stuck half of a hot dog in one of the fingers of my glove. After we batted, I went out to my position, put on my glove, and I felt something slimy in there. I took off my glove and shook it and the hot dog came out, so I took it and fired it toward our dugout. It slid over to a security cop sitting on a chair in front of Steinbrenner.

"George asked the cop what it was and the cop showed him the hot dog, and I remember hearing that he ordered Houk to find out who put the hot dog in my glove and George was going to punish him. Houk just ignored him."

As time went on, Steinbrenner became more and more involved with the Yankees, reneging on his promise "to let the baseball people run the team." He became "the Boss," the most hands-on of owners. Soon, his imprint was all over the Yankees.

He would spare no expense to put a championship team on the field, approving trades and signing free agents Catfish Hunter, Don Gullett, Rich Gossage, and the big prize, Reggie Jackson. The money allocated by Steinbrenner, deemed exorbitant at the time, proved to be a bargain. In his fourth year of ownership, the Yankees won their first pennant in 12 years; in his fifth year, they won their first World Series in 15 years.

During his tenure, Steinbrenner presided over first the renovation of Yankee Stadium and then the construction of a new Yankee Stadium, saw the Yankees become the first American League team to draw 4 million fans at home, and watched his team win 10 pennants and six World Series in 30 years.

Absentee ownership indeed!

Mickey Mantle shows off a home-run ball.

"If I had known it was such a big deal, I'd have done it myself a few times." —Mickey Mantle, commenting on José Canseco's becoming the first player in baseball history to hit 40 home runs and steal 40 bases in the same season

Mantle's Washington Monument

In a magnificent 18-year career, Mickey Mantle hit 536 home runs, every one without benefit of chemical enhancement, every one after baseball ended segregation by opening its doors to men of color, all of them before fences were brought in with the construction of modern facilities, baseballs were souped up, and the strike zone shrank to the size of a postage stamp, most of them before expansion created opportunities for pitchers who were unworthy of the designation "major leaguer."

Of those 536 home runs, some won games, some were meaningless and, therefore, forgettable, and some inched him inexorably up the ladder in career home runs until, by the time he left the game, he had hit more than any player in history save for Babe Ruth and Willie Mays. And a handful of those 536 home runs were so majestic, so incomprehensible in their distance as to establish Mantle as perhaps the most powerful man ever to lace up a pair of spiked shoes.

The granddaddy of all Mantle home runs came early in his career in Washington's old Griffith Stadium on April 17, 1953, in the fourth game of Mantle's third season with the Yankees. It was home run number 37 of his career, and it established him as the premier power hitter of his generation. It also introduced into baseball's lexicon the term "tape-measure home run."

Mantle always said he considered himself a better hitter right-handed than left-handed, but he believed he had more power batting left-handed. While it's true that most of his longest home runs came from the left side of the plate, the biggest one came as a right-handed batter against Senators left-hander Chuck Stobbs, who would win 107 major league games but who would forever be linked with Mantle in this one defining moment of the Switcher's career.

Batting against Stobbs in the fifth inning, the Mick picked out a 1–0 fastball and drove it out of sight. When last seen, the ball was sailing over the fence in left-center field, clear out of the ancient ballpark.

According to legend, Arthur "Red" Patterson, director of public relations for the Yankees, left the press box and trekked to the street beyond the left-field fence, where he discovered a 10-year-old boy who had recovered the baseball. Patterson supposedly asked the boy where the ball had landed, marked the spot, and later carried a tape measure out to the spot to determine the exact distance. He reported his findings: 562 feet.

Skeptics—not the least of whom was Mantle himself—doubted the veracity of Patterson's claim.

Years later, Mantle said, "Red told the writers he went down and found out where the ball landed and measured the distance. Red got a lot of publicity out of that, which was his job. I know I hit it good, but to tell you the truth, I don't think Red ever left the press box."

Mantle did confirm another incident that came with his monster shot.

"Billy Martin was on third base," he said, "and when I hit the ball Billy went back to the bag to tag up. I used to have this habit when I hit a home run of running around the bases with my head down because I didn't want to show up the pitcher.

"So I'm running around the bases with my head down, and when I got near third base, I heard Frank Crosetti [Yankees third-base coach] yelling, 'Look out.' I look up and there's Billy on third base, tagging up. Here I hit the ball clear out of the ballpark, and Billy was tagging up. I never let him forget it."

Scott Brosius hits a game-winning home run in the 2001 World Series.

18. Double Jeopardy

Not once, but twice!

There is nothing in baseball quite so dramatic, quite so exciting, quite so uplifting (or deflating, depending on whether you are on the giving or receiving end) as a game-tying home run in the bottom of the ninth.

When it happens in consecutive games, it is all of the above, and more. It's miraculous.

For the Yankees, this double dagger to the hearts of the Arizona Diamondbacks came on the nights of October 31 and November 1, 2001, in Yankee Stadium.

Seeking their fourth straight World Series championship, and their fifth in six years, the Yankees lost the first two games in Arizona and returned to Yankee Stadium for a critical and emotion-packed Game 3. Just seven weeks after the unspeakable tragedy of 9/11, George W. Bush became the sixth sitting United States president to throw out the first ball at a World Series game.

After the president made his pitch, Roger Clemens and Mariano Rivera took over and held the Diamondbacks to three hits in a 2–1 victory, the Yankees' eighth straight World Series win at Yankee Stadium. But there was still work to be done if the Yankees' run of world championships was to continue.

Things looked bleak for the home side as they batted in the ninth inning of Game 4, trailing, 3–1. Curt Schilling had held the Yankees to three hits over the first seven innings, then gave way to Byung-Hyun Kim, the Korean side-armer who struck out the side in the eighth and retired Derek Jeter on a bunt leading off the ninth.

When Paul O'Neill stroked a single to left, the Yankee Stadium crowd of 55,863, their flickering hopes buoyed, roared their approval, attempting with their voices and their enthusiastic rhythmic applause to will their heroes to some last-ditch miracle.

But Bernie Williams struck out, and the Yankees were down to their final out, one out away from falling behind in the Series, three games to one. Tino Martinez, hitless in nine at-bats for the Series, was up, representing the last chance for the home team.

Martinez swung at Kim's first pitch and drove it over the center-field fence, a prodigious blast, and a timely and dramatic one. The Yankee Stadium crowd went wild in celebration. Kim's shoulders sagged in despair. The score was tied, 3–3.

With two outs in the tenth, Jeter belted Kim's 3–2 pitch over the right-field fence, giving the Yankees a heart-stopping 4–3 win. The Series was even at two games each.

Twenty-four hours after Martinez and Jeter lit up the Bronx night with their home-run heroics, the Yankees, in the first baseball game ever played in the month of November, again found themselves trailing by two runs in the bottom of the ninth. Miguel Batista had stymied the Yankees through seven and two-thirds scoreless innings, holding them to five hits while outpitching Mike Mussina. Greg Swindell got the final out in the eighth, and again the Diamondbacks summoned Kim, who was called in to protect a two-run lead in the ninth.

Jorge Posada led off the bottom of the ninth with a double, and there was hope again in the Bronx. But Shane Spencer grounded out and Chuck Knoblauch struck out, and for the second straight night, the Yankees were down to their final out, in danger of returning to Arizona down three games to two.

This time the last chance was left to Scott Brosius, two-for-12 in the Series, hitless for the night. Brosius took Kim's first pitch for ball one. He swung at Kim's second pitch and sent it high and far to left field, deep into the night and into the seats, to tie the score, 2–2.

Brosius's blast sent the game into extra innings for the second straight night, and this time Alfonso Soriano's single to right in the tenth scored Knoblauch from second with the winning run in a 3–2 Yankees victory.

Although the Yankees went to Arizona and lost the next two games and the World Series, the defeat could not diminish the magnitude of the ninth-inning lightning in Games 4 and 5.

Game-tying two-run home runs with two outs in the bottom of the ninth off the same pitcher, and victories in extra innings, in consecutive games. Who said lightning doesn't strike twice in the same place?

Babe Calls Homer

Did he or didn't he?

Only Babe Ruth knew for sure if he really did call the shot on his home run in Game 3 of the 1932 World Series, and the Babe wasn't talking. When he did talk–depending on when and to whom he did the talking–he took both sides of the debate.

The mighty Bambino was slipping. He was 37 years old, and his waistline was expanding rapidly. He had batted "only" .341, down from a high of .393 nine years earlier, drove in 137 runs, down from a high of 171 11 years before, and hit 41 home runs, down from a high of 60 just five years earlier. Although he finished second in the league in homers, it was the first time in seven seasons he had not reigned as home-run champion of the American League.

What Ruth had going for him was his enormous pride and great motivation against the Yankees' World Series rivals, the Chicago Cubs. There was no love lost between the Yankees and the Cubs to begin with. It stemmed from Yankees manager Joe McCarthy having been fired by the Cubs after the 1930 season and from what the Yankees, and Ruth, considered an insult to shortstop Mark Koenig, their beloved former teammate.

The veteran Koenig had been traded by the Yankees to Detroit in 1930, then was picked up two years later in August by the Cubs for their run at a pennant. Koenig's experience, excellent defense, and .353 average may have been the difference in Chicago's four-game margin over the Pirates.

Despite Koenig's contribution to their pennant, the Cubs voted him only a half share of the World Series money, thereby outraging his former Yankees teammates, Ruth in particular. He called the Cubs cheapskates, and they responded with a savage and blistering verbal attack against Ruth throughout one of the most hostile World Series ever.

The Yankees won the first two games of the Series at home and then traveled to Chicago for Game 3, where the ugliness continued as Cubs fans joined in on the verbal assault.

Charlie Root was the Chicago pitcher, and the Babe wasted no time taking the measure of the veteran right-hander. Batting with two on in the first inning, Ruth delivered a three-run home run that gave the Yankees the early lead.

Ruth batted again in the second and flied out, then came to bat in the fifth with the score tied, 4–4, one out, and nobody on base. What happened next has been the subject of great debate, conjecture, and interpretation to this day. What is fact is that Ruth took a strike, stepped out of the batter's box, pointed toward center field, stepped back in the box, and took a second strike. Again, Ruth stepped out, pointed, and stepped back in. Root's next pitch was a change-up. This time Ruth unfurled a mighty swing, connected with all his abundant weight, and drove the ball high and far, over the wall, into the center-field seats.

By pointing, was Ruth saying he was going to hit a home run?

Did he call his shot?

Or was he simply telling Root ,"That's one…" after the first pitch, and "That's two…" after the second pitch?

Cubs manager Charlie Grimm's version is that Cubs pitcher Guy Bush was needling Ruth from the bench, and the Babe's response was to point to the mound as if to tell Bush, "You'll be out there tomorrow."

Ruth further obfuscated the legend by, at various times, confirming and denying that he had called his home run. During spring training the following year, Ruth attended

Babe Ruth arrives home after hitting a home run in the 1932 World Series.

a dinner party where one of the guests asked him about the "called shot." Sportswriter Grantland Rice chronicled Ruth's response in his book, *The Tumult and the Shouting*:

The Cubs had [bleeped] my old teammate by cutting him in for only a measly, [bleeping] half share of the Series money. Well, I'm riding the [bleep] out of the Cubs, telling 'em they're the cheapest pack of [bleeping] crumbums in the world. We've won the first two, and now we're in Chicago for the third game. Root is the Cubs' pitcher. I park one into the stands in the first inning off him, but in the fifth it's tied, four to four, when I'm up. The Chicago fans are giving me hell.

Root's still in there. He breezes the first two pitches by, both strikes. The mob's tearing down Wrigley Field. I shake my fist after that first strike.

After the second, I point my bat at these bellerin' bleachers, right where I aim to park the ball. Root throws it, and I hit that [bleeping] ball on the nose, right over the [bleeping] fence.

'How do you like those apples, you [bleep, bleep, bleep],' I yell at Root as I head towards first. By the time I reach home, I'm almost fallin' down I'm laughing so hard. And that's how it happened.

Believe it or not, as you wish.

The Yankees went on to sweep the 1932 World Series, which would be the last one in which Ruth played. He left the Yankees three years later, retired a year after that, and passed away 13 years after that. He took with him to his grave his bigger-than-life legend as a man and a basher of baseballs, and the truth about his "called shot."

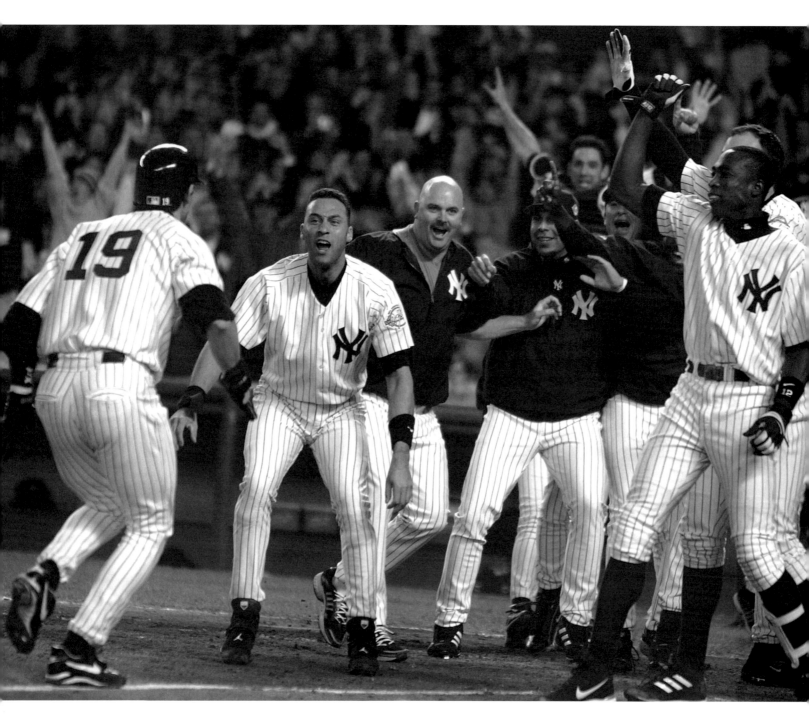

Number 19, Aaron Boone, comes into home to the delight of his teammates.

Boone Goes Boom

Aaron Boone, son of one major league All-Star and brother of another, knew little about baseball's most intense rivalry, the Red Sox and Yankees, and less about curses. He was five years old when Bucky Dent hit his famous home run over Fenway Park's Green Monster that was a dagger to the hearts of Red Sox fans, and he wasn't even a Yankee when the 2003 season began.

But on the night of October 16, in Yankee Stadium, Boone would blast his way into the storied history of this almost century-long blood feud. He would join in tandem with Dent as public enemy numbers 1 and 1A to New Englanders, only slightly less notorious and reviled in Boston than Aaron Burr. Together, they would forever be known in Beantown as Bucky [Bleeping] Dent and Aaron [Bleeping] Boone.

Boone, who had toiled in the shadow of his father, Bob, an outstanding catcher for 16 major league seasons, and his older brother, Brett, had joined the Yankees from Cincinnati without much fanfare on July 31. His arrival hardly caused a ripple in New York or changed the balance of power in the American League East. He became the Yankees' regular third baseman and played in 54 games without great distinction, with a .254 batting average, six home runs, and 31 runs batted in as the Yankees finished six games ahead of the Red Sox in the division.

The two archrivals would hook up again in the ALCS and reach a climactic Game 7 tied at three games each after alternating victories in the first six games. Boone had batted .200 in the four-game division series against Minnesota and was a mere two-for-16 in the first six games of the ALCS, his lack of production so debilitating for the Yankees that he was benched in the seventh game and replaced by Enrique Wilson.

The Red Sox struck early in Game 7, scoring three times in the second inning off former Red Sox star right-hander Roger Clemens and adding a run in the fourth. With a 4–0 lead and their ace, Pedro Martinez, in control (he had allowed two harmless singles over the first four innings), the Red Sox seemed on their way to their first American League pennant in 17 years and, at long last, an end to the fabled "Curse of the Bambino."

Mike Mussina, making his first career relief appearance after 400 consecutive major league starts, gave the Yankees faithful hope by following Clemens with three scoreless innings, while the Yankees scored single runs in the fifth and seventh to trim their deficit to 4–2. But a solo home run by David Ortiz in the eighth boosted Boston's lead to 5–2, which seemed like a mountain for the Yankees to climb in light of Martinez's dominant pitching.

In the bottom of the eighth, the Yankees began to stir: a one-out double by Derek Jeter, an RBI single by Bernie Williams, a double by Hideki Matsui, and a two-run double by Jorge Posada. The score was tied, 5–5, and Martinez was out of the game as the inning continued.

Jason Giambi flied out for the second out, and now the fickle finger of fate reached out and touched Aaron Boone on the shoulder. Ruben Sierra, pinch-hitting for Wilson, was intentionally walked, and Boone was sent in to run for Sierra. The Yankees would fail to score again in the inning, but the score was tied and Boone was in the game, taking over for Wilson at third base, waiting for his date with destiny.

Mariano Rivera, the Yankees' peerless reliever who had saved Games 3 and 5, entered in the ninth and pitched three scoreless innings as they went to the bottom of the eleventh.

Tim Wakefield, whose tantalizing knuckleball had stymied the Yankees in Games 1 and 4, had come in to pitch the bottom of the tenth for the Red Sox. He retired the Yankees in order in the tenth and went out for the eleventh. The first batter for the Yankees in the bottom of the eleventh was Boone.

Wakefield threw his knuckleball…Boone swung… and the ball was sent soaring into the Bronx night, high and far toward the seats in left field. It disappeared into the crowd, just inside the left-field foul pole, as Yankee Stadium erupted in joyous, raucous celebration of the Yankees' 39th American League pennant, only the fifth time in major league history that a postseason series ended with a home run.

As a postscript to history, Boone would tear up his knee in an off-season pickup basketball game and miss the entire 2004 season. In need of a third baseman, the Yankees would engineer a deal with the Texas Rangers that would bring to New York Boone's replacement, Alex Rodriguez.

Lightning Strikes

The stars were out in Yankee Stadium on the night of Saturday, June 17, 1978, but none was shining brighter than Ron Guidry. It was the night the one they called "Louisiana Lightning" hung his star in the Yankees' firmament.

He had navigated a treacherous, mine-filled path to get to this point. Only 15 months before, it appeared his days as a Yankee were numbered. He had been beaten up by the Tigers in an exhibition game, bringing forth rumors that Guidry would be packaged in a trade and sent to another team.

At the time, he was nearing his 26th birthday, and Yankees officials were beginning to despair that Guidry ever would be the pitcher they hoped he could be. True, he was a hard thrower, but he had failed to win a game in two seasons in New York. At 5'11" and 161 pounds, there were doubts that he had the stamina and strength to survive the rigors of pitching in the major leagues.

In later days, the three men who would decide his fate—owner George Steinbrenner, team president Gabe Paul, and manager Billy Martin—each would claim he was the one who insisted on keeping Guidry, it was the other two who wanted to trade him. The truth has never been revealed, but suffice it to say that Guidry remained a Yankee and reinforced an adage as old as baseball itself: The best trades are the ones that are not made.

Guidry began the 1977 season in the bullpen. He pitched five times in relief, won one game, saved another, and impressed Martin enough for the manager to give him a start against the Mariners on April 29. Guidry pitched eight and one-third scoreless innings, allowed seven hits, struck out eight, and was inserted into the starting rotation. He would finish the season with a record of 16–7, five shutouts, 176 strikeouts, and an earned-run average of 2.82. At the age of 27, Ron Guidry had arrived, and he would go to spring training in 1978 as a key member of the Yankees' pitching staff.

By June 17 of that year, as he faced the California Angels, Guidry had emerged as the ace of the Yankees' staff. He had won his first 10 decisions. In his three previous starts, he had pitched two complete games, allowed two runs and 15 hits in 26⅓ innings, and struck out 31.

Guidry started out by striking out two Angels in the first inning and one more in the second. He then struck out the side in the third and fourth. His fastball seemed to have a little extra hop on this night, and his slider was biting down and in viciously on right-handed hitters. When he struck out the side again in the sixth, he had 14 strikeouts, and the Yankee Stadium crowd of 33,482 became increasingly aware it was witnessing something special.

For the first time, the crowd began a ritual that has continued with Yankees pitchers to this day. Whenever Guidry got two strikes on a hitter, the crowd rose as one and began a rhythmic applause in anticipation of strike three.

Guidry struck out one batter each in the seventh and eighth innings, and in the ninth, he struck out Dave Chalk and got Joe Rudi for the fourth time (he struck out Don Baylor, Bobby Grich, and Brian Downing twice each) for his 18th strikeout. He had set a Yankees record, and an American League record by a left-hander, for strikeouts in one game. He held the Angels to four hits in a 4–0 victory, his second consecutive shutout, and improved his record to 11–0 (he would not lose until July 7, in the Yankees' 82nd game).

"I was hurt, and I wasn't playing in that game," said Bucky Dent. "Sitting on the bench, I had a good look at the Angels' batters. They were going up there just trying to foul the ball off. Gator was so overpowering that they were just trying to put the ball in play because he was throwing the ball right by them."

Ron Guidry ices his arm and celebrates with a snack after his 18-strikeout game against the Angels.

Said Guidry about his record performance: "It gave me a lot of personal gratification because you don't get to stand on the mound very often and just strike out people at will. You have to have a lot of lucky things happen in a game like that; guys have to take pitches when they should be swinging, and swing when they should be taking.

"I didn't usually strike out many hitters on called strikes. That was just one of those nights. I'd start a hitter off with a breaking ball, and he'd swing at a ball in the dirt. The next time he'd be taking the first pitch, and I'd throw a fastball right down the middle of the plate and he'd take it. I was fortunate. That's how it went the whole night. Other times, you might throw that same fastball, and they'd way-lay it because that's what they were guessing. That night was just one of those special nights where every time they guessed, it was wrong."

When the game ended, Guidry was almost half-way through one of the greatest seasons any pitcher ever had. He would win 25 games and lose only three (all three defeats to pitchers named Mike—Caldwell of the Brewers, Flanagan of the Orioles, Willis of the Blue Jays). He would lead the league in wins, winning percentage (.893), earned-run average (1.74), and shutouts (nine), and finish second to Nolan Ryan in strikeouts (260 to 248).

Don Mattingly was among the top 10 in American League home runs in 1985 and 1986.

Donnie Baseball

Don Mattingly could do it all.

Selected by the Yankees as an Indiana high school senior in the 19th round of the June 1979 free-agent draft, he had become "Donnie Baseball," the "Hit Man," known in the vernacular of baseball as "a pure hitter." His 238 hits and 53 doubles in 1986 are the most ever by a Yankee in a single season (he would finish his career fifth to Lou Gehrig, Babe Ruth, Mickey Mantle, and Joe DiMaggio on the Yankees' all-time list in hits, second to Gehrig on their all-time list in doubles).

In the years from 1984 to 1987, many proclaimed Mattingly the best player in the game. In those four seasons, he was first, third, second, and fifth in the American League in batting; first, second, first, and seventh in hits; fifth, first, third, and fifth in RBIs; and fifth, first, second, and seventh in Most Valuable Player voting. And he was the peerless first baseman, with three Gold Gloves in those four years.

For all he achieved, one would be hard pressed to find Mattingly's name on any list of home-run hitters. His 35 homers in 1985 (fourth in the American League) and 31 in 1986 (sixth in the AL) were the only times in a 14-year career he was among the top 10 in the American League in home runs, yet his most memorable moments in a brilliant career came in a home-run-hitting binge in an eight-game stretch over 11 days in July 1987.

It began in Yankee Stadium on July 8 in the first inning against Mike Smithson of the Minnesota Twins. Rickey Henderson led off with a single, Gary Ward followed with a single, and Mattingly deposited one into the right-field seats, his ninth home run of the season. In the sixth inning of the same game, Mattingly hit number 10, a solo shot off Juan Berenguer.

The following day, against the Chicago White Sox, Mattingly connected in the sixth inning off Richard Dotson.

He hit another on July 10, a grand slam in the second inning against Joel McKeon, and another on July 11, a solo homer off Jose DeLeon in the third inning, and still another on July 12, against Jim Winn for Mattingly's 14th home run of the season.

He had hit a home run in each game of the four-game series against the White Sox, and he had hit home runs in five consecutive games. In those five games, Mattingly had 11 hits in 23 at-bats, 12 RBIs, and six home runs.

As hot as he was, Mattingly would have liked to press on, but if opposing pitchers couldn't cool him off, perhaps the schedule could. The annual All-Star Game, played in the Oakland Alameda County Stadium, interrupted his hot streak. Mattingly, the American League's starting first baseman, batted three times. He reached on an error in his first at-bat and walked his next two times at the plate.

After the three-day All-Star hiatus, the Yankees journeyed to Texas to resume the season with a four-game series against the Rangers, and Mattingly picked up right where he had left off. In the second inning of the first game of the series, he belted a grand slam off knuckle-baller Charlie Hough for his 15th home run of the year. The following night he connected off Paul Kilgus in the sixth inning. He had hit home runs in seven consecutive games, one short of the major league record. Dale Long, like Mattingly a left-handed-hitting first baseman who would later play for the Yankees, had done it in 1956 as a member of the Pittsburgh Pirates.

On July 18, Mattingly faced Juan Guzman and, in his first at-bat, grounded to the first baseman. But leading off the fourth, Mattingly hit Guzman's third pitch over the left-field fence, just over the outstretched glove of Rangers left fielder Ruben Sierra.

With a chance to break Long's record the next night, Mattingly grounded to the pitcher, singled to center, and lined to first against Greg Harris, and then he doubled to left against reliever Jeff Russell as the Yankees were crushed by the Rangers, 20–3.

The streak was over. Not only had Mattingly tied Dale Long's major league record, but he had also accomplished what no other Yankee ever had–not Ruth or Gehrig, Mantle or Maris, Joltin' Joe or Mr. October–he hit home runs in eight consecutive games.

Billy's Ball

I played in four World Series and each one was against the Brooklyn Dodgers. We'd go into the Series, and the newspapers would always compare the two teams, position by position. I would be compared with Jackie Robinson or Jim Gilliam, and the papers always gave the Dodgers a big edge at second base.

The photographers would be on the field before the game, taking pictures of Joe DiMaggio, Mickey Mantle, Whitey Ford, Hank Bauer, Gene Woodling, and Gil McDougald, and ignoring me. I'd say to them, "Hey, you'd better take my picture because I'm going to be the star of this thing."

"We don't need you, Billy," they'd say.

"Okay," I'd say. "Go ahead and leave me out. But you're going to come looking for me to take my picture and I'm going to be too busy."

—Billy Martin

Billy Martin never lacked confidence. He was brash. He was cocky. He was egotistical. He was outspoken. And he backed it all up with his play. In short, Billy Martin was a winner.

Martin joined the Yankees in 1950, and they won the World Series. He was a Yankee in 1951, 1952, and 1953, and they won the World Series all three years. In 1954, Martin was in the army. The Yankees finished second in the American League to the Cleveland Indians.

He returned to the Yankees for 20 games in 1955, and they won the pennant. He was a Yankee in 1956, and they won the World Series. He was traded midway through the 1957 season. The Yankees won the pennant but lost the World Series to the Milwaukee Braves in seven games.

Martin played for the Yankees in parts of seven seasons, and they won the pennant all seven years. He played in five World Series, and the Yankees won four of them.

His lifetime batting average during the regular season was .257; in the World Series, his average was .333.

During the regular season, he hit 64 home runs in 3,419 at-bats, or one homer for every 53.4 at-bats; in the World Series, he hit five home runs in 99 at-bats, or one in every 19.8 at-bats.

During the regular season, he had 333 RBIs, or one for every 10.3 at-bats; in the World Series, he had one RBI for every 5.2 at-bats.

In the 1952 World Series, Martin batted .217, hit one home run, and drove in four runs. In comparison, Robinson, the Dodgers' second baseman, batted .174, hit one home run, and drove in two runs.

In the 1953 World Series, Martin set a record for a six-game Series with 12 hits, batted .500, hit two home runs, and drove in eight runs; Gilliam, the Dodgers' second baseman, batted .296, hit two home runs, and drove in four.

In the 1955 World Series, Martin batted .320 and drove in four runs; Gilliam batted .292 and drove in three.

In the 1956 World Series, Martin batted .296, hit two home runs, and drove in three runs; Gilliam batted .083, did not hit a home run, and drove in two.

But Martin's most memorable World Series moment came not with his bat, but with his glove, his head, and his heart. And it came in 1952, when he had his lowest World Series batting average.

The Dodgers won Game 1 of the Series at Ebbets Field, 4–2, on Duke Snider's two-run homer in the sixth, but the Yankees came back to take the second game, 7–1, as Martin highlighted a five-run sixth with a three-run homer.

Back home, the Yankees dropped the third game, 5–3, when Pee Wee Reese scored from third and Robinson from second on a passed ball in the ninth by Yogi Berra.

Again the Yankees came back tie the Series with a 2–0 victory in Game 4 behind Allie Reynolds's four-hitter.

The win-lose, win-lose pattern continued in Game 5, with the Dodgers winning, 6–5, in 11 innings. Carl Erskine, who allowed all five Yankees runs in the fifth, went the distance for the win. That sent the Dodgers home to Ebbets Field for the final two games, needing one win to capture their first World Series.

But once more the Yankees rebounded to tie the Series, winning 3–2 despite two more home runs by Snider. That set up the climactic, winner-take-all seventh game on October 7.

Eddie Lopat, the loser in Game 3, started for the Yankees. For the Dodgers, it was Joe Black, a rookie right-hander who had relieved in 54 games during the regular season and started only two. But he was the surprise starter and winner in Game 1 of the World Series, and the starter and hard-luck loser in Game 4. Now he was making his third start in seven days.

The Yankees broke a scoreless tie with a run in the fourth on a double by Phil Rizzuto and an RBI single by Johnny Mize, but the Dodgers rallied in the bottom of the inning. When they loaded the bases with no outs, Yankees manager Casey Stengel replaced Lopat with Reynolds, who had started Games 1 and 4 and saved Game 6 in relief. The Dodgers tied the score on Gil Hodges's sacrifice fly, but Reynolds kept the score tied by striking out George "Shotgun" Shuba and getting Carl Furillo to ground out.

Woodling's leadoff home run in the fifth broke the tie, but the Dodgers came right back in the bottom of the fifth to tie the score again on a double by Billy Cox and a single by Reese.

Mantle broke the tie with a home run in the sixth and then singled home a run in the seventh to put the Yankees up, 4–2.

To preserve the lead, Stengel brought in Vic Raschi to start the seventh. Raschi had pitched a complete-game victory in Game 2 and had been the winning pitcher in Game 6, the day before, going seven and two-thirds innings.

By calling on Raschi, Stengel had used every one of his Big Three–Lopat, Reynolds, and Raschi, who had combined for 46 wins in the regular season–in this seventh game.

In the bottom of the seventh, the Dodgers rallied against Raschi, loading the bases with one out. With Snider and Robinson due up, and the tying and go-ahead runs on base, Stengel took a daring (some called it desperate) gamble. He brought in Bob Kuzava, a journeyman left-hander who was 8–8 during the season, had a career record 40–32 for six major league seasons, and had not appeared in the first six games of the World Series.

"I always hit Kuzava well when I faced him in the minor leagues," Snider said years later. "As he was taking his warm-up pitches, I walked over to Jackie in the on-deck circle and said, 'Well, Jack, we've been waiting for this for a long time, and it's up to you and me. I'd just as soon get it over with.'

"'Yeah,' Jackie said. 'I'd like to see you get it over with, too. Whack one, and get us two or three runs.'"

The count went to 3–2 on Snider, who fouled off a few pitches before getting under one and lifting it in the air to third baseman McDougald.

"I was disappointed," said Snider, "but I returned to the bench confident Jackie would get a hit and drive in the tying runs."

With right-handers warming up in the bullpen, Stengel surprisingly stayed with the left-hander, Kuzava, against Robinson, a deadly right-handed hitter.

Said Kuzava, "I thought I'd been there just to get Snider out and that I was home free. After all, Casey still had Johnny Sain in the bullpen and he'd faced Robinson in the National League, and Ebbets Field was death for left-handed pitchers.

"But when the old man got to the mound, he said to me: 'Okay, let's get Robinson, too, and get out of this inning.'

"I'll never understand why Casey chose to go against the book like he did, but I have to feel good about the fact he obviously had a lot of faith in me. That was the only time I ever faced Robinson."

Billy Martin catches Jackie Robinson's wind-blown fly ball during Game 7 of the 1952 World Series.

Once again, the count went to 3–2, which meant all three Dodgers runners would be off with the pitch. A single would mean two runs and a tie score. A double would bring home three runs and give the Dodgers the lead.

Kuzava fired a fastball in on Robinson's hands, and Robinson hit a towering pop fly on the infield. For an instant, everything came to a halt. Nobody was moving except the Dodgers runners, racing around the bases. Joe Collins, the Yankees' first baseman, never moved. Apparently, he had lost the ball in the sun.

Suddenly, Martin was streaking from his second-base position, past the pitcher's mound, heading toward the third-base foul line. Somewhere between the mound and the foul line, between home plate and third base, Martin was racing as fast as he could, his cap flying off his head as he reached out at the ball hurtling from the sky. Leaning, straining, reaching on the dead run, he caught the ball at his knees as it was about to fall to the ground.

Kuzava pitched the eighth and ninth innings and did not allow a hit, completing the 4–2 victory, and the Yankees had won their fourth consecutive World Series.

"I have no idea how Martin caught that ball," said Snider. "I still don't know. But he did."

There is no mystery. It was simply Martin, quicker thinking and more alert than most, coming through once again in the clutch.

24. The Boston Massacre

On September 7, 1978, the Yankees arrived in Boston for a four-game series in Fenway Park trailing the Red Sox by four games, a position that, in light of previous events, was both a remarkable turnaround and a moral victory.

Just seven weeks before, the Yankees were 14 games behind Boston, and in the intervening weeks they had been beset with turmoil, turbulence, unrest, and controversy.

- Billy Martin, after uttering his infamous statement about Reggie Jackson and owner George Steinbrenner that "One's a born liar, and the other's convicted," had been fired and then seven days later had been rehired for the 1980 season.
- The Bronx Zoo had run amok, its denizens having taken over the compound from the zookeepers.

Into this maelstrom came Bob Lemon to provide a steadying hand that righted the Yankees' listing ship. He had taken over as manager from Martin, promising the players he'd let them play and "I'll try to stay out of the way."

As important as Lemon's laid-back approach was, the key to the Yankees' surge was the return of their injured players.

"We had a lot of injuries early in the season," said Bucky Dent. "Catfish [Hunter] was hurt, Mickey Rivers was out, I was out. A bunch of guys were hurt, then, all of a sudden, we started getting one guy back, then another, and the Red Sox started getting hurt a little bit."

"We were 14 games ahead," said Red Sox relief pitcher Bob Stanley, "and then [Rick] Burleson got hurt and [Fred] Lynn got hurt. We lost every game at home to teams from the West Coast, and I remember Yaz [Carl Yastrzemski] saying, 'We're going to blow this.' Burleson and Lynn were very important to our club, especially Burleson."

The Red Sox had built their huge lead, in part, on the backs of their chief rivals from New York. They took two out of three from the Yankees in June, swept a two-game series in Yankee Stadium in August, and held a 6–2 season edge on the Yankees. But by September 7, their surge had left the Yankees in striking distance of the Red Sox. A sweep of the four games in Fenway, unlikely as it seemed, would nonetheless move them into a first-place tie.

The Red Sox were in prevention mode. A split of the four-game series would leave them still four games ahead of the Yankees with only 20 games remaining.

"We went into Boston on a Thursday, and it was the weirdest feeling," Dent remembered. "We were four games back, and there was a different intensity about how our club came out, the way we went about our business. You could feel it, and you could sense it."

It started immediately, the Yankees spraying hits all over Fenway Park. Mike Torrez, who would be the pitcher on a fateful day in Boston three weeks later in the "Bucky Dent Playoff Game," started for the Red Sox and failed to get an out in the second inning. The Yankees scored two runs in the first and banged out five hits in the second, all singles, to score three more. They added two runs in the third inning and five more in the fourth.

"One's a born liar, and the other's convicted." —Billy Martin, talking about Reggie Jackson and owner George Steinbrenner, who was convicted of a felony for making illegal campaign contributions to President Richard Nixon. As a result of his remark, Martin was forced to resign as manager of the Yankees during the 1978 season.

The Yankees outscore the Boston Red Sox 42–9.

After three and a half innings, the Yankees led, 12–0. They had 15 hits, 13 of them singles. Willie Randolph, their leadoff hitter, batted three times before the Red Sox's ninth-place hitter batted once.

Catfish Hunter started for the Yankees, but still not fully recovered from his early-season shoulder injury, he lasted only three innings. Ken Clay, a young right-hander who earlier in the season had been criticized by Steinbrenner for "spitting the bit" in a start against the Red Sox, replaced Hunter and pitched six solid innings for the win, a 15–3 blowout. The Yankees amassed 21 hits, 16 singles, and never hit a ball over the friendly left-field wall, the so-called Green Monster.

The Yankees picked right up in the second game of the series, pounding out 17 more hits (this time they hit two home runs, a three-run shot by Reggie Jackson, and a solo blast by Lou Piniella, who also doubled and tripled) in a 13–2 rout.

In the third game, Ron Guidry pitched a 7–0 complete-game two-hitter for his 21st win, and in the fourth game, the Yankees pounded out 18 more hits, all singles, and finished the debacle with a 7–4 victory.

The Yankees had completed the four-game sweep. After a long struggle, they had drawn even with the Red Sox in the 142nd game of the 162-game season. They started hitting and never stopped. In the four games, the Yankees outscored the Red Sox, 42–9, and out hit them, 67–21, and 57 of the Yankees' 67 hits were singles.

"When we swept them," said Dent, "it was like, 'We're going to beat these guys. We got it now.' We knew we were going to win."

The newspapers called the sweep "the Boston Massacre," and on the Freedom Trail, in Faneuil Hall and the Old North Church, on Bunker Hill, in Lexington and Concord, the Yankees had replaced the Red Coats as public enemy number one.

David Wells follows in Don Larsen's footsteps and pitches a perfect game.

25. Wells...and Good

The similarities and coincidences between them were too obvious to ignore. They attended the same San Diego high school. They were known as much for their erratic lifestyles as for their ability to throw a baseball. And they both reached the pitcher's pinnacle, the ultimate, 42 years apart.

Both Don Larsen and David Wells also had come to the Yankees from Baltimore, Larsen in an 18-player trade in 1954, Wells as a free agent 42 years later.

And both would pitch a perfect game.

A perfect game—27 batters up, 27 batters down, not one reaching first base in any manner, by hit, walk, or error—is the rarest of baseball feats. It has come along, since the start of the modern era, once every eight years; it has occurred once in approximately every 16,000 games.

Larsen pitched his perfect game in Yankee Stadium in the fifth game of the 1956 World Series against the Brooklyn Dodgers—it was then, and remains to this day, not just the only perfect game, but the only no-hitter in World Series history—some seven months after he was discovered at 5:30 one morning in St. Petersburg, Florida, with his car wrapped around a telephone pole.

Wells's perfect game was not so dramatic or on so big a stage. His came in Yankee Stadium on May 17, 1998. Five years later, Wells would contend in his autobiography that he pitched his gem hung over after a night of revelry. And it would be revealed that he was a 1982 graduate of San Diego's Point Loma High School, the same school Larsen had attended a half century before.

Wells, a burly, pot-bellied left-hander whose idea of a training regimen was to walk to his local tavern and throw down a few cold ones, had been a Yankees nemesis as a member of the Toronto Blue Jays. His immense girth belied the fact that he was an agile athlete gifted with a rubber arm, and a polished pitcher who relied as much on guile and an ability to out-think batters as on his pinpoint control and devastating curveball.

In addition, Wells was something of a baseball historian and memorabilia collector who idolized Babe Ruth. Unable to wear Ruth's retired No. 3, Wells opted for No. 33, doubling the Babe's famous number. He also purchased, at considerable cost, a baseball cap worn by Ruth and wore it on the mound.

With the Yankees, Wells flourished. In his first season in pinstripes, he won 16 games, a career high, and followed that up with a 5–1, five-hitter over Cleveland in the American League Division Series. His crowning achievement would come in his eighth start in 1998.

Wells's perfect game, against the Minnesota Twins, was as seamless as any ever pitched. Sandy Koufax, who pitched four no-hitters, one of them a perfect game, in his brilliant career, once said, "You need luck to pitch a no-hitter. The batters must hit the ball in the right direction, and you need the fielders behind you to make the plays."

Ordinarily, to complete a no-hitter, or a perfect game, a pitcher must survive several close calls: line drives hit right at fielders, great plays made behind the pitcher, drives that hook foul at the last instant. Not so in Wells's case. On this day, the Twins never had a chance. There were no hard-hit balls, no close calls, no great defensive plays that preserved the perfect game.

Wells, who would win 18 games and lose only four during the season and win four more without losing in the playoffs and World Series, struck out 11 Twins and had no anxious moments, no close calls, in putting down 27 batters in order.

The pitching masterpiece was completed when Pat Meares hit a lazy pop fly to right field that nestled softly in Paul O'Neill's glove. Wells leaped in the air in celebration, and his teammates rushed to the mound to greet him, then carried the rotund left-hander off the field.

He had pitched only baseball's 13th perfect game and, including Larsen's, only the second in Yankees history. The Yankees had waited 42 years since their last perfect game. They wouldn't have to wait quite that long for their next one.

David Cone continues the Yankees' streak of successful and talented pitchers.

26. A Perfect Match

Perhaps it was merely the power of suggestion.

On July 18, 1999, the Yankees were honoring one of their bigger-than-life heroes. It was Yogi Berra Day at Yankee Stadium.

The lovable Berra, a Yankees treasure who had produced so magnificently in a 19-year Hall of Fame career, had been estranged from the team since being fired as its manager 14 years before. He vowed never to return to Yankee Stadium as long as George Steinbrenner owned the team.

But Steinbrenner extended an olive branch, visited Berra at the New Jersey museum named for the former catcher, and the two men buried the hatchet and put the past in the past. To commemorate their reconciliation, Steinbrenner offered to arrange this day in Berra's honor.

Yogi Berra Day was a joyous occasion at Yankee Stadium. The guest of honor was showered with gifts and with love and affection pouring out from the packed stands from grateful fans. His grandchildren, most of whom were not even born the last time Berra set foot in Yankee Stadium, were there to hear their grandpa being lauded for his exploits as a Yankee, the three Most Valuable Player awards, the 2,150 hits, the 358 home runs, and especially the 14 pennants and 10 World Series championships in his 19 years.

Among Berra's many Yankees teammates invited to attend was Don Larsen, who had combined with Berra for one of the greatest moments in baseball history, the only perfect game pitched in the World Series 43 years before.

In a highlight of the ceremonies, that moment was re-created, Larsen pitching, Berra catching the final out, and then leaping in the arms of the pitcher in celebration, just as he had done that October afternoon in 1956.

When the ceremonies were concluded, the Yankees took the field against the Montreal Expos in an interleague game. On the mound for the Yankees was David Cone, who was born seven years after Larsen's perfect game. Cone was winding down a distinguished career. He had won 179 major league games, nine already that season. But he had never pitched a no-hitter, although he had come close several times.

Three years earlier, in the month of May, Cone had suffered an aneurysm in his right arm that threatened his career. He underwent surgery and began a lengthy rehabilitation, determined to pitch again, and returned to the mound against the Athletics in Oakland on September 2, 1996.

It was a miraculous recovery, all the more because through seven innings, Cone had not allowed a hit. He could have continued pitching and might even have been able to complete his no-hitter, but manager Joe Torre chose to err on the side of caution. Rather than risk further injury to the right-hander, Torre removed Cone from the game in the eighth inning. There would not be a no-hitter for David Cone that day. But there would be a second chance three years later, with Berra and Larsen there to see it.

Against the Expos, Cone was economical and efficient as he set down the Montreal hitters one after another. He also was fortunate.

"You gotta call a blacksmith."
—Yogi Berra, giving advice to Billy Martin after Martin locked his keys in his car

As so often happens in games like these, Cone had a good deal of help from his defense and from the baseball gods:

- A diving catch of a line drive by right-fielder Paul O'Neill in the first inning
- A diving stab of a blistering groundball up the middle by second baseman Chuck Knoblauch in the eighth
- A fly ball to left field in the ninth that was bobbled by Ricky Ledee, who recovered and caught the ball just as it was about to fall to the ground

When Orlando Cabrera hit a foul ball to third baseman Scott Brosius for the final out, David Cone had pitched not only his first no-hitter, he had pitched, fittingly, a perfect game.

Cone had retired all 27 Expos batters using only 88 pitches. He struck out 10 and never reached a three-ball count on any batter.

Only 14 months after another pitcher named David (Wells) had pitched the second perfect game in Yankees history, Cone had pitched the third. And he did it in the presence of the man who pitched the Yankees' first perfect game, Don Larsen.

27. New Game in Town

This newfangled game, known at the time as "base ball," was catching on. People seemed to enjoy it. What's more, businessmen, taking careful note that people were more than willing to spend their money to watch men play the game, saw it as a means to an end: a way to expand their already-ample bank accounts.

By the turn of the 20th century, the National League of Professional Base Ball Clubs, since its inception in 1876, had enjoyed a monopoly in the major cities of the United States. The time had come to challenge that monopoly, and the man to do it was Ban Johnson, president of the Western League, the strongest minor league in the 1890s. In concert with Charles Comiskey, owner of the St. Paul franchise, Johnson took steps to strengthen his league with an eye toward competing on equal footing with the established National League.

Johnson declared war by convincing his owners to open their checkbooks and entice the National League's biggest stars to jump to the Western League. They succeeded in luring away Cy Young, John McGraw, "Wee" Willie Keeler, Ed Delahanty, Jesse Burkett, and the biggest star of all, Napoleon Lajoie, whom Connie Mack seduced into signing with his Philadelphia team by offering him a munificent salary of $6,000, almost three times as much as the National League's mandatory salary maximum.

By 1901, the new American League was ready to challenge the National League, and it opened for business with eight teams: the Boston Americans, Detroit Tigers, Philadelphia Athletics, Baltimore Orioles, Washington Senators, Cleveland Blues, Milwaukee Brewers, and Comiskey's Chicago White Sox, which he moved from St. Paul.

The new league was an immediate success, but President Johnson realized there was something missing: his league had no team in the nation's largest and most vital city, New York, where the Giants of the National League had an even stronger monopoly than the National League had enjoyed in its first quarter of a century.

National League owners could not overlook the fact that in its first year, the new league attracted more fans than the old league in the three cities in which they competed head-to-head–Philadelphia, Chicago, and Boston–or that in its second year, the American League drew 2,228,000 fans to the National League's 1,684,000.

In an effort to put an end to the price war, and the escalation of players' salaries, the National League agreed to a truce and full acceptance of the new league. The only demand made by the National League was that the new league promise not to put a team in Pittsburgh. Johnson complied. His league would stay out of Pittsburgh. But there was no agreement to keep his league out of New York.

The Giants, whose owners had strong connections in New York City government, fought their own battle to retain their monopoly and threatened to have a streetcar line run over second base at any American League ballpark site. Meanwhile, Johnson, still determined to have a New York franchise in his league, was busy seeking prospective New York owners with political influence of their own. To that end, he came upon Frank Farrell, a former saloonkeeper and wealthy gambling entrepreneur, and William Devery, a former New York City police chief, who had amassed a fortune in real estate and by allegedly accepting payoffs for turning a blind eye to illegal activities.

Johnson arranged for Farrell and Devery to purchase the Baltimore franchise for $18,000 and move it to New York. The new owners spent an additional $300,000 to build Hilltop Park, a 10,000-seat stadium on Broadway and 168th Street, the present site of Columbia Presbyterian

The Highlanders play ball
at Hilltop Park in 1909.

Hospital. They hired Clark Griffith away from the White Sox as manager, giving him carte blanche to spend what it took to bring the best players available to New York in order to compete with the rival Giants.

Griffith raided the National League for such stars as infielder Wid Conroy, catcher Jack O'Connor, outfielder Keeler, and pitchers Jack Chesbro and Jesse Tannehill.

The new team in town was called the Highlanders, in part because Hilltop Park was one of the highest elevations in Manhattan and in part to capitalize on the popularity of Gordon's Highlanders, a prominent British military unit of the day.

The Highlanders (they would be renamed Yankees and move from Hilltop Park to the Polo Grounds 10 years later) played their first game in Washington on April 22, 1903, and lost to the Senators, 3–1. Chesbro was the losing pitcher.

Player/manager Griffith, still an effective pitcher, won 14 games, Chesbro and Tannehill combined for 36 wins, and Keeler batted .318, fifth in the league. The Highlanders nevertheless still finished fourth, 17 games behind, as fate would have it, the Boston Americans, proving a truism that would be repeated many times in the future: Money does not buy championships.

Graig Nettles' sharp wit was almost as good as his fielding.

"He went from Cy Young to *sayonara*."

—Graig Nettles, on the trade of Sparky Lyle by the

Yankees to the Texas Rangers in 1978, one year after

Lyle won the American League Cy Young Award

28. Batman…and Robbin'

His bat was one of the main reasons the Yankees reached the World Series in 1978. His glove was the main reason the Yankees won their second consecutive World Series.

Graig Nettles combined with Reggie Jackson to give the Yankees a potent one-two power punch during the regular season. His 27 home runs tied Jackson for the team lead; his 93 RBIs were four less than Jackson's team-best total.

But it was Nettles's gifted glove that took center stage in the World Series against the Los Angeles Dodgers: the glove upon which he inscribed E-5 (the scorekeeper's symbol for error, third baseman) in self-deprecating humor.

Around the Yankees, Nettles was renowned for his acerbic wit:

- "The best thing about being a Yankee is that you get to see Reggie Jackson play every day; the worst thing about being a Yankee is that you get to see Reggie Jackson play every day."
- "Most kids grow up dreaming to play for the Yankees or being in the circus. I'm lucky. I got to do both."
- "If they want somebody to play third base, they have me. If they want somebody to attend banquets, they can get Georgie Jessel."
- "Sparky Lyle went from Cy Young to *sayonara*." (Lyle was traded by the Yankees one year after winning the Cy Young Award.)

The 1978 Series opened in Dodger Stadium, and, in the comfort of their own home, cheered on by their own fans, the Dodgers won the first two games, a commanding two-games-to-none lead in the best-of-seven Series. When the Series shifted to Yankee Stadium for Game 3, the Yankees were in trouble and in need of a lift. Nettles gave it to them with his glove. He ripped the heart out of the Dodgers with his defense.

The Yankees led 2–0 in the third inning, when the Dodgers rallied against Ron Guidry. The Dodgers had one run in and a runner on first with two outs when Reggie Smith ripped a blistering smash inside the third-base line. Reacting quickly, Nettles left his feet, dove toward the foul line, and grabbed the ball on the backhand as it was about to rattle into the left-field corner. Nettles got up and fired a strike to first base, nailing Smith, saving a run, and preserving the Yankees' lead.

The score remained 2–1 in favor of the Yankees as the Dodgers batted in the fifth and put runners on first and second with one out. This time Smith hit a line drive headed for left field, when Nettles appeared out of nowhere to knock the ball down, saving at least one run and loading the bases.

Next up was Steve Garvey, who hit a wicked smash inside third, the ball again headed for left field. And again Nettles dove, grabbed the hot shot, and fired to second for the inning-ending force.

> **"The best thing about being a Yankee is you get to watch Reggie Jackson play every day. The worst thing about being a Yankee is you get to watch Reggie Jackson play every day." —Graig Nettles**

In the sixth, the Dodgers loaded the bases with two outs when Davey Lopes hit another smash inside third. One more time Nettles grabbed it with a backhanded stab and fired to second for the inning-ending force.

In a display of third-base magic reminiscent of the incomparable Brooks Robinson of Baltimore in the 1970 World Series against Pittsburgh, Nettles saved at least five runs as the Yankees won the game, 5–1, and turned the Series around.

"They can stop shooting," said Lopes. "They have enough highlights for the film already."

Nettles had changed the momentum of the World Series with his glove. The Yankees went on to win the next three games and capture their second straight championship. And there was little doubt the outcome would have been different had Nettles not been able to come up with just one of the four hot smashes off Dodgers bats in the third game.

"Nettles was good in Minnesota and he was good in Cleveland, but he didn't get his due until he went to New York," said Robinson, the standard by which all third basemen are measured. "When he made all those great plays in the World Series, and he got the recognition because now you had non-baseball fans watching the games. Everybody was amazed at the plays he made, but the teams he played against knew he had been doing those things all the time."

Taking the Fifth

Imagine how the history of baseball, and the Yankees, might have been altered if George Weiss did not have the courage of his convictions.

It was Weiss, general manager and architect of the Yankees dynasty of the 1940s and 1950s, who brought Casey Stengel in to manage the team, an unpopular choice that was greeted with skepticism and scathing criticism at the time.

When Bucky Harris was fired after the 1948 season, Weiss proposed Stengel as Harris's successor, a choice that brought strong opposition from the team's co-owners, Dan Topping and Del Webb.

The owners' doubts were understandable. Stengel's entire major league career, 14 years as a player, nine years as a manager, had been spent in the National League. He was too old, 59, and he had a dismal résumé as a major league manager.

With the Brooklyn Dodgers from 1934 through 1936, and the Boston Braves from 1938 through 1943, Stengel had been a complete failure—two fifth-place finishes, two sixths, and five sevenths in his nine seasons, only once finishing above .500.

In Boston, he was under constant vicious attack from sardonic *Boston Record* columnist Dave Egan, known as "the Colonel." Prior to the 1943 season, Stengel was struck by a car and incapacitated with a broken leg. Summing up the season, Egan wrote, "The man who did the most for baseball in Boston in 1943 was the motorist who ran Stengel down two days before the opening game and kept him away from the Braves for two months."

What's more, Stengel had a reputation as a clown, best remembered, despite a productive playing career, for such antics as arriving at the ballpark one day, doffing his cap, and having a sparrow fly free. It was hardly the image Topping and Webb wanted for their dignified, reserved, and businesslike Yankees.

But Weiss knew another Stengel. They had been friends for some 40 years, and Weiss regarded Stengel as a knowledgeable baseball man, one who ate, slept, and breathed the game and would talk about it for hours on end. Weiss argued that in Brooklyn and Boston, Stengel had inferior playing talent. He pointed to the job Casey did in winning the Pacific Coast League championship with Oakland in 1948 and insisted his friend would be a success with the Yankees.

Weiss had wanted to bring Stengel in to manage the Yankees after Joe McCarthy resigned in 1946, but Larry MacPhail, then a one-third partner of Topping and Webb, opposed the idea. Harris was MacPhail's choice, and he proved to be a favorite with Yankees players and fans but not with Weiss. When MacPhail sold out his interest after the 1947 season and the Yankees slipped to third in 1948, Weiss saw his chance to replace Harris and bring in Stengel.

Weiss began campaigning for Stengel by first working on Webb, convincing him that Stengel was the right man for the job. Webb then took the general manager's arguments to Topping, who, somewhat reluctantly, eventually fell in line.

On October 12, 1948, the day after the final game of the World Series between the Cleveland Indians and Boston Braves, in New York's chic 21 Club, Stengel was introduced as the manager of the Yankees. At a gathering of the city's baseball press, Topping stood behind a podium and said, "I'm happy to make the announcement that Casey Stengel has been appointed manager of the New York Yankees."

There was a smattering of applause from the writers in attendance, most of whom had covered Stengel as a player for the Giants and Dodgers and later as a manager.

They knew him well and liked him. As John Drebinger of *The New York Times* said, "If you didn't like Stengel, you didn't like anybody."

Stengel appeared nervous when he took the microphone, which may have been the last time he ever was nervous talking to anyone. He thanked "Bob" Topping, referring to the Yankees' co-owner's playboy brother, a misidentification that would come to be known as a Stengel trait. He rarely remembered names, frequently misspelled or mispronounced them, and often referred to acquaintances and even close friends simply as "Doctor."

Asked about his new team, Stengel said, "I never had players like this."

The New York writers treated the selection of Stengel favorably, a view not shared by all members of the nation's press. In Boston, Dave Egan, the Colonel, wrote, "Well, sirs and ladies, the Yankees have now been mathematically eliminated from the 1949 pennant race. They eliminated themselves when they engaged Perfesser Casey Stengel to mismanage them for the next two years, and you may be sure that the perfesser will oblige to the best of his unique ability."

In spring training, some writers noted that Stengel seemed in awe of the talent around him and overwhelmed by the enormity of his task. Joe DiMaggio, never a Stengel fan, took one writer aside one day and confided that the new manager seemed "bewildered."

If there was one thing on which Stengel had unanimous approval, however, it was his ability to handle, develop, and bring along young players. He was regarded as an excellent teacher who was not afraid to entrust important assignments to rookies. Circumstances required Stengel to make immediate changes to the Yankees. First baseman George McQuinn had retired after the 1948 season, so Stengel moved right fielder Tommy "Old Reliable" Henrich to first base. He made Yogi Berra his everyday catcher. And he gave important assignments to three rookies, outfielders Hank Bauer and Gene Woodling, and second baseman Jerry Coleman.

Stengel's biggest problem, however, was the absence for the first 65 games of the season of his team's biggest star, best player, and leader, DiMaggio, because of a heel injury. This caused Stengel to employ what would be his greatest managerial skill—the ability to maneuver his players by instituting a seldom-used platoon system: right-handed batters against left-handed pitchers, left-handed batters against right-handed pitchers. Bobby Brown and Billy Johnson shared third base, Woodling and Bauer alternated in left field or right field, and Cliff Mapes and Johnny Lindell were platooned in center until DiMaggio returned.

His first season as manager of the Yankees was Stengel's most brilliant. He held his team together in the face of DiMaggio's absence and a rash of injuries to other important players and directed his team to the pennant by sweeping the final two games of the season against the Red Sox, with his greatest detractor, Colonel Egan, as a witness. Stengel's year was complete when the Yankees won the World Series from the Dodgers in five games.

In 1950, Lindell was sold to the Cardinals, and infielder George "Snuffy" Stirnweiss was traded to the St. Louis Browns. Three newcomers joined the Yankees, one of them a skinny second baseman whom Stengel had managed in Oakland and loved for his combativeness and his fierce desire to win. Casey suggested to Weiss that he purchase the contract of the tough guy, and Billy Martin became a Yankee. Joe Collins took over as the regular first baseman with Henrich, now 37 years old, becoming a part-time player. In midseason, the Yankees called up from their Kansas City farm team a young left-handed pitcher named Whitey Ford, who would win nine of 10 decisions in the stretch run to the Yankees' second straight American League pennant.

The Yankees finished three games ahead of the Tigers and then won the 1950 World Series from the Philadelphia Phillies in a four-game sweep.

Two seasons, two pennants for Stengel, and eight wins in nine World Series games. Stengel was now solidly entrenched as manager of the Yankees, and there no longer was any doubt about his ability to lead.

Stengel holds court in the Yankees' locker room.

The 1951 season brought more changes. Henrich retired. Pitcher Tommy Byrne and outfielder Mapes were traded to the St. Louis Browns. Third baseman Billy Johnson was traded to the St. Louis Cardinals. Former star relief pitcher Joe Page was released. Newcomers to the Yankees were infielder Gil McDougald and a teenage Adonis from Oklahoma with awesome power as a switch-hitter, the speed of an Olympic sprinter, and a Li'l Abner physique. His name was Mickey Charles Mantle.

DiMaggio was hampered by age and injury, Mantle was having trouble connecting with American League pitching, and Ford was serving a two-year hitch in the army, but somehow the Yankees managed to win their third consecutive pennant mainly because of their pitching big three of Vic Raschi, Allie Reynolds, and Eddie Lopat, who combined for 59 wins. The Yankees finished five games in front of the Cleveland Indians and beat the cross-town rival New York Giants, four games to two, in the World Series.

With that championship came the end of another era. After 13 fabulous seasons, DiMaggio retired.

Despite the loss of their greatest star, there was no panic for the Yankees. Stengel's genius was now accepted, and confidence abounded that he could continue to succeed despite the great one's absence.

Stengel was now solidly in command of the Yankees' fortunes, and with his success, his popularity skyrocketed. He was a character who became a favorite among photographers because of his distinctive, photogenic face and his willingness to mime and mug for the camera, and with writers because of his riveting stories, his baseball acumen, and his colorful language. Perhaps inadvertently, perhaps to avoid revealing his true thoughts, he engaged in a form of doublespeak that became known as "Stengelese."

He would interrupt a conversation or begin a monologue by poking a gnarled finger at his listener and saying, "Now, wait a minute, doctor." In Stengelese, nothing ever began, it "commenced"; a player, or a manager, was never fired or released, he was "discharged"; a Baltimore chop, or a high bouncer to the infield, was a "butcher boy"; a rookie or an inexperienced person was "like Ned in the third reader"; and someone who had passed on was "dead at the present time."

Upon DiMaggio's retirement, Stengel was asked for his evaluation of the famed Yankee Clipper.

"He's the best I've ever had," he said, but it wasn't Stengel's way to let it go with a simple declarative statement. He continued: "Now, wait a minute, for crissakes. You're going into too big a man. Maybe he woulda been an astronaut if he wanted. He could hit some balls off the moon and see if they'd carry. There were a lot of great ones, and Ruth could pitch, too, but this fella is the best I had. About DiMaggio, you don't have to falsify anything. He started in with a bang and never stopped. Of course, when he played for me he was handicapped, but you wouldna knowed it if you didn't see him limping in the cabs and in the clubhouse. The best thing he had—and I'll give you a tip—was his head. He saw some of the faults of the pitcher, and he would hit—the ball and he didn't just hit on Sunday, neither."

Doubts that the Yankees could win without DiMaggio's leadership were soon dispelled. They finished three games ahead of Cleveland in 1952 to win their fourth consecutive pennant, and then beat the Dodgers in a seven-game World Series.

In search of an unprecedented fifth straight world championship, the Yankees welcomed Whitey Ford back from military service in 1953, and he led the pitching staff with 18 wins. For the third straight year, the Yankees beat out Cleveland to win the pennant. For the second straight year, they faced the Brooklyn Dodgers in the World Series. This time, the Yankees took care of the Dodgers in six games.

Stengel was perfect as a Yankees manager—five seasons, five pennants, five world championships, a record that might never be matched.

30. Terry and the Giants

Ralph Terry had waited two years for this, two years since he threw the pitch that resulted in one of the classic moments in World Series history.

It came in the bottom of the ninth of the seventh game of the 1960 World Series in Forbes Field, Pittsburgh. Terry threw the pitch, Bill Mazeroski hit it over the left-field fence, and the Pirates had won their first World Series in 35 years.

For two years, Terry had lived with the ignominy of that one pitch, and now he had his chance for redemption.

The 1962 season had been a breakout one for Terry, a tall, handsome, 26-year-old Oklahoman. He had led the American League in victories with 23. A workhorse, he had started 39 games, pitched in relief in four other games, logged 298⅔ innings, and teamed with Whitey Ford to form a solid one-two pitching punch that accounted for 40 wins and was instrumental in helping the Yankees win their third straight pennant, by five games over the Minnesota Twins.

In the World Series, the Yankees opposed the Giants, their one-time intercity rivals who had fled New York for San Francisco four years before. The Giants were a formidable foe, powered by such future Hall of Famers as Willie Mays, Willie McCovey, Orlando Cepeda, and Juan Marichal.

Ford drew the Game 1 assignment in San Francisco and beat the Giants, 6–2. Terry got the nod for the second game and, while he pitched well–two runs and five hits, including a home run by McCovey, in seven innings–he was the hard-luck 2–0 loser as Jack Sanford muffled the Yankees' bats on three hits.

Back in New York, they split the next two games and Terry opposed Sanford again in Game 5. This time Terry had the upper hand. With the score tied, 2–2, in the eighth, Tom Tresh blasted a three-run homer to put the Yankees ahead. Terry survived a Giants rally in the ninth to win, 5–3, and give the Yankees a three-games-to-two lead as the Series returned to Northern California.

Back in San Francisco, the World Series was put on hold because of a torrential downpour that caused a three-day delay in the Series. As a consequence of the deluge, both managers, Ralph Houk of the Yankees and Alvin Dark of the Giants, were able to rearrange their pitching rotation to allow their best to finish out the Series.

Game 6 matched Ford with another veteran left-hander, Billy Pierce, who was brilliant in throwing a three-hitter for a 5–2 victory over the Yankees and Ford that left the Series tied, three games apiece.

Now it all came down to a climactic seventh game with Terry and Sanford matched up for the third time, each having won once. Both starters pitched masterfully, the Yankees breaking through for a run in the fifth when Tony Kubek hit into a double play with the bases loaded.

Going into the bottom of the ninth, Terry had allowed just two hits, a single by Sanford with two outs in the sixth after Terry had retired the first 17 Giants, and a two-out triple by McCovey in the eighth.

Matty Alou led off the bottom of the ninth pinch-hitting for relief pitcher Billy O'Dell and beat out a bunt. Terry then struck out Felipe Alou and Chuck Hiller, leaving the Yankees one out away from the championship. But Mays drilled a shot into the right-field corner that looked like it would bring home the tying run. Playing right field for the Yankees, Roger Maris reacted quickly. He raced toward the foul line to cut the ball off before it reached the fence, whirled quickly, and fired a strike to the cutoff man, second baseman Bobby Richardson. Alou was held up at third. It was, at least temporarily, a game-saving play by Maris.

The next batter was McCovey, a powerful left-handed hitter and one of the most feared home-run hitters in the game, who had tripled and homered against Terry in the Series. But a long ball wasn't needed. A single would win the game and the World Series for the Giants.

Houk visited the mound to talk to Terry. Would the manager replace the right-hander with a lefty? He had Ford warming up in the bullpen, along with Bud Daley and Marshall Bridges, also left-handed.

Houk decided to stay with Terry, leaving himself open to second-guessing if McCovey delivered a game-winning hit. Thoughts of Mazeroski's Series-winning home run off Terry just two years earlier flashed in the minds of many in the Candlestick Park crowd of 43,948, especially when McCovey teed off on a pitch from Terry and sent it high and far toward the right-field fence. But the ball hooked foul.

Later, Terry would say he didn't think history had repeated itself.

"Where I threw that ball," he said, "to hit it good, he had to hit it foul."

Again, Terry pitched and McCovey swung and sent a vicious line drive headed toward right field but also right at second baseman Richardson, who grabbed the blistering line drive chest high for the final out.

It was vindication for Terry and another world championship for the Yankees.

Ralph Terry and the Yankees beat the Giants, 1–0, in Game 7 of the 1962 World Series.

31. Tommy Gun

He came out of Massillon, Ohio, the town that produced football legend Paul Brown, coach/part owner of the Cleveland Browns. The son of German immigrants, Tommy Henrich signed with his hometown team, the Cleveland Indians, as a 21-year-old before the 1934 season.

Because of a glitch in his contract, he was granted free agency by Commissioner Kenesaw Mountain Landis on April 14, 1937, a portent of things to come, decades before Marvin Miller, the Major League Players Association, George Steinbrenner, Reggie Jackson, Jason Giambi, and multimillion-dollar contracts. Seven teams vied for his services, but five days after earning his freedom, he signed with the Yankees, his favorite team when he was a boy.

With the Yankees, he played right field and joined with center fielder Joe DiMaggio and left fielder Charlie "King Kong" Keller to form what many have called the greatest outfield in baseball history.

Henrich would play 11 seasons for the Yankees and help them win four American League pennants and World Series, and he would play a supporting role in some of the most memorable events the game has known.

It was with a bat borrowed from Henrich that DiMaggio got the hit that broke George Sisler's modern-day hitting streak of 41 games.

It was Henrich who was at bat when Brooklyn Dodgers catcher Mickey Owen let a game-ending third strike get past him in Game 4 of the 1941 World Series, allowing the Yankees to rally for four runs to win the game and, eventually, the Series.

And it was Henrich who was stationed in right field in Brooklyn's Ebbets Field in Game 4 of the 1947 World Series when pinch-hitter Cookie Lavagetto broke up Bill Bevens's no-hitter in the bottom of the ninth with a shot off the right-field fence, and over Henrich's head.

His career statistics—a .282 average, 183 home runs, 795 runs batted in—belied an uncanny ability to come up big in crucial situations, a deadly hitter with the game on the line. That ability for big hits earned Henrich the nickname "Old Reliable" from announcer Mel Allen because of situations like this:

Game 1 of the 1949 World Series in Yankee Stadium, another of those classics between the Yankees and the Brooklyn Dodgers. Henrich, now 36 years old and nearing the end of his excellent career, had been reduced to a part-time player. Beset by an inordinate number of injuries and in need of a replacement for George McQuinn, who had retired, first-year Yankees manager Casey Stengel needed someone to play first base. He chose Henrich, aging and slowed by the years.

In 115 games, 52 of them at first base, Henrich's bat had still been productive. He batted .287 with 24 home runs and 85 RBIs (the following year he would play in only 73 games, 34 at first base, bat .272, hit six home runs, drive in 34 runs, and retire at season's end), and was a key figure in helping the Yankees win the pennant by sweeping the final two games of the season against the Red Sox in Yankee Stadium.

Now he was at first base for the opening game of the World Series, a pitching masterpiece between Brooklyn's 23-year-old Don Newcombe, the National League Rookie of the Year who had won 17 games for the Dodgers, and Allie Reynolds of the Yankees, also a 17-game winner.

Through eight innings the game was scoreless, with neither pitcher giving an inch. Newcombe had allowed four hits and struck out 11. Reynolds had allowed two hits and struck out nine.

When Reynolds retired the Dodgers in order in the top of the ninth, the Yankees came to bat in the bottom half

Tommy Henrich lives up to his nickname, "Old Reliable."

of the inning. Scheduled to lead off was Henrich, who had been held in check by Newcombe in his first three at-bats: a ground ball to short in the first, a pop fly to short in the third, a soft fly ball to center field in the sixth.

The first two pitches to Henrich by Newcombe, who had not walked a batter, were out of the strike zone. With the count 2–0 and Yogi Berra and DiMaggio hitting behind him, Henrich knew Newcombe was determined not to put

the winning run on base. Henrich was certain Newcombe would throw him a fastball, and he would be ready for it.

Newcombe threw a fastball. And Henrich was ready for it. He ripped into it and sent a low line drive toward the right-field stands. The ball sailed over the head of Dodgers right fielder Carl Furillo and landed in the lower right-field seats to give the Yankees a 1–0 victory.

"Old Reliable," indeed.

Mystique, Aura, and the Kid

One of the most glorious periods in Yankees history began in 1996 with the arrival of Joe Torre as manager, a choice initially met with scorn, derision, doubt, and skepticism.

Over the next five seasons, the Yankees would win five American League East titles, four pennants, and four World Series, and they would do it in such magical fashion as to evoke a popular myth that the Yankees were fortified with two additional weapons. Their names were Mystique and Aura.

All great runs of success must have a beginning, and the Yankees' came on the night of October 9, 1996. After dispatching the Texas Rangers, three games to one in the division series, the Yankees took on the Baltimore Orioles in Game 1 of the American League Championship Series in Yankee Stadium. There were angels in the outfield for the Yankees that night, including one cherubic 12-year-old from New Jersey named Jeffrey Maier.

Andy Pettitte started for the Yankees against Scott Erickson, and two breaks—a fly ball by the Yankees' first batter of the game lost in the background by left fielder B.J. Surhoff, and a botched double play on a bad throw by shortstop Cal Ripken Jr.—allowed the Yankees to score single runs in the first and second innings, a sign of things to come.

With single runs in the second, third, fourth, and sixth, the Orioles took a 4–2 lead. But in the seventh, the Yankees got a third break and a third run when Bobby Bonilla crashed into the right-field wall and was unable to hold on to a drive by Bernie Williams.

In the bottom of the eighth, the Orioles fortified their defense to preserve their one-run lead. Mike Devereaux took over for Surhoff in left field, and Tony Tarasco replaced Bonilla in right. Jim Leyritz led off the inning by striking out against Baltimore reliever Armando Benitez.

That brought up Derek Jeter, who was completing a sensational rookie season and who had singled in his first two at-bats in this game. Jeter got into a Benitez fastball and

sent a line drive deep to right field. Tarasco went back to the wall quickly and was poised to catch the drive when out of nowhere came Maier, who had the foresight to bring his baseball glove to the game. He reached out and stretched his glove over the railing. The ball nestled in the youngster's mitt just before Tarasco could grab it.

Right-field umpire Rich Garcia signaled home run. The Orioles protested vehemently, arguing that the youngster's hand had reached over the rail into the playing area, thereby preventing Tarasco from making the catch. Jeter, the Orioles insisted, should be called out.

The argument was to no avail. The umpires gathered to discuss the play and agreed there was insufficient evidence to support the Orioles' contention. The call stood, the game was tied, and Orioles manager Davey Johnson was ejected from the game.

They went into extra innings. Mariano Rivera, not yet the greatest postseason closer in baseball history, pitched a scoreless tenth and eleventh.

Leading off the bottom of the eleventh, Williams hit an undisputed game-winning home run, giving the Yankees a 5–4 victory.

The Yankees would go on to beat the Orioles in five games, and they would win the World Series in six games over the Atlanta Braves.

Reflecting on Jeter's critical, game-tying "home run" in the eighth inning of Game 1 of the ALCS, Tarasco would say, "In my mind, there's no way I would have dropped it. Merlin must have been in the air."

On this night, Merlin, taking the form of a 12-year-old from New Jersey named Jeffrey Maier, had joined Mystique and Aura to comprise a Big Three that would lead the Yankees to the first of four World Series triumphs in Joe Torre's first five years as manager of the Yankees.

"I want to thank the good Lord for making me a Yankee." —Joe DiMaggio

Fan Jeffrey Maier reaches out to save the day.

33. Joe's Tee-Off Party

After finishing in third place in 1948, behind Boston and Cleveland, the Yankees fired manager Bucky Harris and replaced him with Casey Stengel, who began his tenure severely handicapped. The Yankees' biggest star, Joe DiMaggio, their inspirational leader who had batted .320 the previous season and led the American League with 39 home runs and 155 RBIs, was injured.

A painful bone spur on his right heel, and a subsequent operation, had caused DiMaggio to miss the first 65 games of the 1949 season. In his absence, Stengel had proved to be remarkably resourceful and creative. Deftly deploying his forces in a platoon system (right-handed hitters against left-handed pitchers, left-handed hitters against right-handed pitchers) Stengel had managed to steer the Yankees into first place despite the loss of DiMaggio. Somehow, the Yankees held a four-and-a-half-game lead over the Philadelphia Athletics, five ahead of the Red Sox when they went to Boston for a three-game series on June 28.

For weeks, reporters had been asking Stengel when DiMaggio would return to the lineup.

"When Joe feels as though he wants to come back, I will put him in the lineup," was Stengel's standard reply.

"I knew when I was coming back, but I wasn't talking," DiMaggio would say years later. "I was pointing for the series in Boston. We would play there only one more time, and I wasn't going to give up that Boston ballpark [Fenway Park]. What better place to make my comeback?"

Secretly, DiMaggio began getting himself ready, taking batting practice at Yankee Stadium in the morning before his teammates arrived for that day's game.

"For four days I hit," DiMaggio said. "Gus Niarhos caught, and Al Schacht [a former major league pitcher, later renowned as the "Clown Prince of Baseball" and at the time a noted New York restaurateur], 60 years old by then, pitched

batting practice. We got some ballboys and batboys to shag. I thought I got myself into fairly decent shape. I knew I was going to play in Boston, but nobody else did.

"I flew up to Boston the day of the game and went right from the airport to the ballpark. I put on my uniform and went out on the bench. The players were on the field and Stengel had his back to me, talking to the writers. He hadn't put up the starting lineup and the writers were asking him about it.

> **"There may be some kid in the stands seeing me play for the first time. I owe him my best."** —Joe DiMaggio, in response to a reporter who asked if there ever was a time he didn't feel like playing

"'I can't give you the lineup yet,' he was saying, and he kept turning around to look at me. I didn't say a word. I just kept tying my shoelaces. He kept looking at me, and finally I gave him a nod and he said, 'Now I can give you the lineup.'"

The comeback was amazing, the baseball equivalent of General MacArthur returning to Corregidor. DiMaggio hit a single and a two-run home run in the first game, won by the Yankees, 5–4.

In the second game, the Red Sox jumped out to a 7–1 lead, but DiMaggio hit two home runs to lead the Yankees to a 9–7, come-from-behind victory.

In the third game, he homered again, a two-run shot in a 6–5 victory that completed a sweep of the three-game series and dropped the Red Sox eight games back.

In his comeback, DiMaggio had powered the sweep by hitting four home runs and driving in nine runs.

The Red Sox would stage a comeback of their own, closing the gap on the Yankees. When they came to Yankee Stadium for the final two games of the season, they had inched ahead in the race and led the Yankees by one game. The Red Sox needed just one win in the final two games to clinch their second pennant in three years.

The Yankees won the first game, which was Joe DiMaggio Day at Yankee Stadium, and then they won the final game of the season to capture their first of five straight championships in Stengel's first five years as manager.

In 76 games, DiMaggio hit 14 home runs, drove in 67 runs, and batted .346, three points higher than the league leaders, George Kell of Detroit and Ted Williams of Boston, but he lacked enough at-bats to qualify for what would have been his third batting championship.

34. A Whitewash

As he warmed up to start Game 4 of the 1961 World Series against the Reds at Cincinnati's Crosley Field, Whitey Ford, already with eight World Series victories, more than any other pitcher, knew he was on the verge of making more World Series history. With three straight World Series shutouts, Ford needed to pitch three more scoreless innings to break a Series record for consecutive scoreless innings by a pitcher—a record that had stood for 43 years.

In 1918, a 23-year-old Boston left-hander named George Herman Ruth, nicknamed "Babe," had shut out the Chicago Cubs in the first game of the World Series and pitched seven scoreless innings in Game 4. Added to 13⅔ scoreless innings against the Brooklyn Dodgers in 1916, that gave Ruth 29⅔ scoreless innings of World Series pitching and broke the record set by Christy Mathewson of the New York Giants.

Mathewson had pitched three consecutive shutouts against the Philadelphia Athletics in the 1905 Series and then added a 28th consecutive scoreless inning in Game 1 of the 1911 World Series, also against the Athletics.

Ford had begun his streak with shutouts in Games 3 and 6 of the 1960 World Series against the Pittsburgh Pirates and has always regretted a managerial decision by Casey Stengel that prohibited Ford from starting more than two games against the Pirates.

By 1961, Stengel was gone, replaced by Ralph Houk, a new manager with new ideas. As his pitching coach, Houk had chosen Johnny Sain, who believed that pitchers should work more frequently, not less. Sain's theory was predicated on the belief that pitchers improve their arm strength by throwing frequently.

"One night I went to Madison Square Garden for a St. John's college basketball game," said Ford. "Houk happened to be there, and at halftime I went over to say hello to him. He mentioned that he was toying with the idea of having me pitch every fourth day instead of every fifth and asked me how I felt about it.

"I told him I was all for it. I always believed I pitched better with only three days' rest between starts instead of four."

When the season started, Houk's plan was in place. Pitching every fourth day, Ford had the best season of his career, a record of 25–4, an earned-run average of 3.21, three shutouts, a league-high 283 innings, and a personal high of 209 strikeouts. Although he completed only 11 of his 39 starts, that was largely due to the presence of Luis Arroyo, a 34-year-old relief pitcher from Puerto Rico the Yankees had obtained from Cincinnati the previous year. Featuring a baffling screwball, Arroyo appeared in 65 games, led the American League with 29 saves, and won 15 more in relief.

The 1961 season was one of the best in Yankees history, the '61 team often called the greatest team ever. Roger Maris and Mickey Mantle, the M&M Boys, engaged in a home-run battle, with Maris winning out after Mantle missed most of the final weeks with an injury. Maris broke Babe Ruth's hallowed single-season home-run mark with 61, Mantle hit a career-high 54 homers, the Yankees as a team set a major league record with 240 home runs. Elston Howard batted .348, and the Yankees won 109 games and finished eight games ahead of the Detroit Tigers.

The Yankees' World Series opponents would be the Cincinnati Reds, who had won their first National League pennant in 21 years.

Ford got the assignment for Game 1 in Yankee Stadium and picked up right where he left off in the regular season. Arroyo wasn't needed, as Ford shut out the Reds on two hits for a 2–0 victory on home runs by Howard and Moose Skowron. It was not only Ford's record eighth World Series victory, but it was also his third consecutive Series shutout.

The Yankees and Reds split the next two games, and it was Ford's turn to pitch again in Game 4, on three days' rest, needing three more scoreless innings to break the record. He retired the Reds in order in the first two innings. In the third, he got Gordon Coleman on a ground ball to second, gave up a hit to former Yankee Darrell Johnson, then retired pitcher Jim O'Toole on a force-out and Elio Chacon on a grounder to second. The record was his.

The streak continued as Ford worked a scoreless fourth and fifth, but when the sixth inning started, he was out of the game. Batting in the third inning, Ford had fouled two balls off his ankle. As the game continued, the ankle began to swell. By the fifth inning, Ford's ankle was throbbing, the pain unbearable. After Ford completed the scoreless fifth, Houk watched him limp off the mound and told Whitey he was finished for the day.

"I'm bringing Jim Coates in to finish the game," Houk said.

Ford had set a World Series record, still held, by pitching 32 consecutive scoreless innings (he would give up a run in the first inning of his next Series start, Game 1 of the 1962 World Series).

After the game, reporters clustered around Ford's locker to question him about his record. Noting that Maris had broken Ruth's single-season home-run record and that he had broken Ruth's World Series record for consecutive scoreless innings, Ford said, "Babe had a bad year in 1961."

Smoke Signals

World War II was over, and baseball looked forward to a boom period, on the field and at the box office, with the return of its great stars. The year was 1946, and the Yankees were filled with optimism, in large measure because of the return of their greatest player, Joe DiMaggio, and their All-Star shortstop Phil Rizzuto, plus the addition of two newcomers, Vic Raschi, a promising right-handed pitcher, and Larry Berra, a squat, oddly shaped catcher from St. Louis with an equally odd nickname, "Yogi."

At the box office the Yankees had the greatest year in their history, attracting 2,265,512 customers to Yankee Stadium, an increase of 1,328,666 over the previous year. But the success at the gate was not matched on the field.

DiMaggio batted .290 and drove in 95 runs, hitting below .300 and failing to reach 100 RBIs for the first time in his career. Rizzuto, who had batted .307 and .284 in his first two seasons before the war, fell to .257. And the rookies proved they were not yet ready for prime time, Berra spending all but seven games with the Yankees' Triple A team in Newark and Raschi winning only two games.

After 35 games, manager Joe McCarthy, in a dispute with team ownership, quit suddenly. A team in turmoil, the Yankees struggled to win 87 games and finished third in the American League, 17 games behind Boston.

With a new manager, Bucky Harris, hired for 1947, Yankees general manager George Weiss set about to fix what was broken. He decided that the team's highest priority was to rebuild a pitching staff that was growing old. Their only pitcher who performed up to expectations was 20-game winner Spud Chandler, and he was 38 years old.

A week after the World Series between the Red Sox and the St. Louis Cardinals, Weiss huddled with representatives of the Indians, who had expressed interest in acquiring Yankees second baseman Joe Gordon, a perennial,

but aging, All-Star. In exchange for Gordon, the Indians were willing to part with one of their starting pitchers, and they submitted a list of three names from which the Yankees could choose one. They were:

Red Embree, age 30, with a career record of 15–22, 8–12 in '46

Steve Gromek, age 27, with a career record of 37–34, 5–15 in '46

Allie Reynolds, age 32, with a career record of 51–47, 11–15 in '46

Weiss's choice was Embree, but first he wanted to check with his best hitter, DiMaggio. Presented with the three names, DiMaggio responded without hesitation.

"Get Reynolds," he said, emphatically. "He gives me fits."

That was good enough for Weiss. If the great DiMaggio had trouble with Reynolds, what chance did mere mortals have?

"You can observe a lot by watching." —Yogi Berra

The trade was made on October 19, 1946, and it paid immediate dividends. In his first season as a Yankee, Reynolds became the ace of their pitching staff. He started 30 games, pitched in relief in four other games, led the team with 19 wins and the American League with a winning percentage of .704 (a 19–8 record), and helped the Yankees win the pennant by 12 games over Detroit. In the World Series against the Dodgers, won by the Yankees in seven games, he went the distance to win Game 2.

By 1949, Reynolds was joined by Raschi and Eddie Lopat to form a Big Three that would help the Yankees win an unprecedented five straight World Series. Part Cherokee, Reynolds picked up the nickname "Super Chief" and a reputation as a fierce competitor and a durable performer who was ready to pitch both as a starter and as a reliever and frequently was called upon to do both. In that five-year run, he made 130 starts, pitched in relief 56 times, and won 83 games. (By way of comparison, in the same period, Gromek won 35 games, and Embree won 18 games and was out of baseball by 1950.) In the World Series during that stretch, Reynolds won four games as a starter and had two wins and four saves as a reliever.

But it was in 1951 that Reynolds wrote his name into the record book with not one but two no-hitters two and a half months apart.

On July 12 in Cleveland, he was matched up against his former teammate, roommate, and friend from his Indians days, Bob Feller, the author of three no-hitters himself. Neither pitcher would yield in the early going, and through the first five innings, neither had allowed a hit. The game's first hit came in the sixth inning off Feller, but Reynolds continued to hold the Indians hitless. A home run by Gene Woodling, another former Indian, gave the Yankees a 1–0 lead in the seventh.

Still, Reynolds carried on. He retired the Indians in the seventh and the eighth. When he put down the Indians without a hit in the ninth, Reynolds had pitched only the fourth no-hitter in Yankees history, the first in 13 years. It was Reynolds's 10th win of the season, his fifth shutout. Feller allowed four hits and was the losing pitcher in the 1–0 duel.

Exactly two months, two weeks, and four days later, on September 28, the Yankees, needing one win to clinch their third consecutive American League pennant, hosted the slugging Red Sox in a doubleheader. In the first game, Reynolds opposed left-hander Mel Parnell. The Yankees put the game away early with two runs in the first inning, two more in the third, and one in the fourth, and then added two more in the sixth.

Now the crowd of 38,038 was focused on the pitching of Reynolds, who had not allowed a hit. He carried an 8–0 lead and his no-hitter into the ninth inning and retired the first two batters, bringing up the redoubtable Ted Williams, who was completing another remarkable season, his 10th straight with a batting average over .300.

"I was very much aware of the no-hitter," Reynolds said years later. "All I had to do was get out Ted Williams. Most times I tried to walk the damn guy. In my opinion it was just stupid to let an outstanding hitter like him beat you."

This time, instead of walking Williams, Reynolds went right after him. Throwing nothing but heat, he got ahead in the count with a called strike on a fastball. On his second pitch, another fastball, Williams lifted a high pop fly behind home plate. Berra settled under it, with Reynolds standing nearby in support. The ball descended into Berra's mitt…and popped out of the glove. Reynolds tried to grab it but couldn't, and it fell safely to the ground as Berra sprawled in the dirt and searched for a hole in the ground in which to disappear.

"Don't worry," said Reynolds, helping Berra to his feet. "We'll get him next time."

Berra returned to his position behind home plate, and Williams was ready with some words for the catcher.

"You put me in a hell of a spot," Williams said. "You blew it, and now I've got to bear down even harder even though the game is decided and your man has a no-hitter going."

Reynolds's next pitch was another fastball in the same spot as the previous one, and Williams again lifted a foul pop behind home plate, in almost the same spot as the first one; it was another chance for Berra who, nervously, waited for the ball to descend. Again it hit in the pocket of his glove. This time he held on to it, squeezed it, and "Super Chief" Allie Reynolds had become the first American Leaguer to pitch two no-hitters in the same season.

36. Mickey Turns Barney to Rubble

Not even the most pessimistic of Yankees observers could foresee 1964 as a last hurrah. Despite a season of turmoil and controversy, and rapidly encroaching age to most of their top players, the Yankees, with a late-season push, managed to win their fifth consecutive American League pennant.

Having won three pennants and two World Series in his first three years as manager, Ralph Houk had been kicked upstairs into the Yankees front office as general manager after the 1963 season.

To replace him in the dugout, Houk's handpicked choice was his old teammate, Yogi Berra, who had served Houk as a coach. It was a bold choice because Berra had no managing experience, but it was a popular one with fans and players. Everybody loved Yogi.

But the Yankees sputtered out of the gate under Berra, losing four of their first five games. By June 10, they had climbed four games over .500, but they were in third place and doubts began to creep into the minds of some that the beloved Berra was capable of leading men. He was too soft, charged his critics. His old teammates, his friends, were taking advantage of Berra's good nature.

A July spurt moved the Yankees back into contention, but on August 17, they went to Chicago to begin a four-game series with the White Sox. Four days later they had fallen back to third place, four and a half games behind the White Sox, who had regained first place. That's when Mary had a little lamb and the normally implacable Berra had a cow.

It was Sunday, August 20. The White Sox had beaten the Yankees, 4–0, completing a four-game sweep. After the game, the Yankees clubhouse was somber as the men showered and dressed, preparing for a trip to Boston for three games against the Red Sox.

Slowly, the Yankees climbed into the bus waiting outside Comiskey Park to take the team to O'Hare Airport.

One by one, the Yankees boarded, most of them with their heads hanging down, embarrassed at being swept by the White Sox, dejected at the prospect of the pennant slipping from their grasp.

Berra was already on the bus, sitting in his customary "manager's seat" in the front, when Phil Linz came aboard. Linz was a blithe spirit, fun-loving and flaky. On the trip, he had purchased a harmonica and some learner's sheet music, and for the past week, he had been teaching himself to play the harmonica. He saw no reason not to continue practicing while waiting for his teammates to board the bus, so he pulled out his sheet music and started playing "Mary Had a Little Lamb."

Berra was from the old school. When you lose, you don't play music, you don't sing, you don't laugh. When you lose, you sit quietly.

"Hey, Linz," Berra shouted to the back of the bus. "Take that harmonica and stuff it."

"What did he say?" Linz asked Mickey Mantle.

"He said play louder," Mantle replied.

Obediently, Linz played louder, and Berra rose from his seat and headed to the back of the bus, fire in his eyes.

"I said take that harmonica and stuff it," said Berra, angrier than most Yankees had ever seen him.

"Do it yourself," said a defiant Linz, flipping the harmonica toward Berra, who swiped at it and knocked it into Joe Pepitone's leg. All hell broke loose as Pepitone began limping around, feigning injury to his leg. Linz was shouting at Berra, who was shouting at Linz. Mantle retrieved the mouth organ and began tooting it.

"That's it for our manager," Mantle said. "From now on, I'm the manager. Here's the signal for the bunt... toot.... Here's the signal for the steal...toot, toot."

By now, everybody on the bus was laughing, including Berra. The whole thing was over as quickly as it started.

It wasn't a major incident, more humorous than serious, but in some ways it served to clear the air and loosen the tension. It would come to represent a turning point and a rallying cry to the Yankees' season.

The Yankees would lose the first two games in Boston and fall six games out of first place on August 22, their low point of the season. But then they won 12 of their next 16 games to right their ship.

Sparking the resurgence was the pitching of a rookie right-hander and the hitting of a veteran superstar. Mel Stottlemyre had been brought up from Richmond of the International League on August 11 and would win nine of his 12 starts. After a slow start, Mantle caught fire and finished with a .303 average, 35 homers, and 111 RBIs. It would be the last productive season of his Hall of Fame career.

On September 16, the Yankees beat the Angels to move a half game out of first. They won again the following day and took over first place by percentage points. They would win their next nine games, giving them an 11-game winning streak that put them four games in front with eight games to play. They had to survive a late-season slide to hold on and finish a game ahead of the White Sox, clinching their fifth straight pennant on the next-to-last day of the season.

On the same day, four teams were still alive for the National League pennant in one of the closest races in history. The Cardinals came through to win the pennant and were matched with the Yankees in the World Series. They had met four times before, the last in 1943, and each team had won twice.

The Series opened in St. Louis, and the first two games were split, the Cardinals beating Whitey Ford, 9–5, in Game 1, the Yankees evening the Series when Stottlemyre beat Bob Gibson, 8–3, in Game 2.

The scene shifted to Yankee Stadium on October 10 for Game 3, which turned into a pitching duel between a couple of 18-game winners, veteran left-hander Curt Simmons for the Cards, and right-hander Jim Bouton for the Yanks.

The Yankees pushed across a run in the second, and the Cardinals tied it with a run in the fifth, and that's how it stood through eight innings. Bouton had allowed six hits, Simmons four, but when the Cards put runners on first and second with one out in the ninth, Simmons was lifted for pinch-hitter Bob Skinner. Bouton preserved the tie by getting Skinner on a drive to deep center and Curt Flood on a line drive to right.

When the Yankees came to bat in the bottom of the ninth, on the mound for the Cardinals was their closer, Barney Schultz, a knuckleball pitcher who had saved 14 games in the regular season, fifth most in the National League.

Scheduled to lead off the bottom of the ninth was Mantle, who had grounded out, walked, and doubled in three previous times at bat but who had always had success hitting against a knuckleball pitcher.

As he prepared to bat against Schultz, Mantle turned to his friend, Ford, and uncharacteristically predicted, "This game is over!"

Schultz threw one pitch to Mantle. And Mantle drove it deep into the right-field seats to give the Yankees a 2–1 victory. It was his 16th World Series home run. He would hit home runs in Games 6 and 7, giving him a record 18 World Series homers, but the Yankees would lose in seven games and would have to wait 12 years before reaching the World Series again.

37. Bare Knuckles

In their illustrious history, the Highlanders/Yankees had won more championships, set more records, and put more players in the Hall of Fame than any other team. Eleven Hall of Famers who had worn the uniform of the Highlanders/Yankees had been pitchers, Babe Ruth not included.

Yet for all their unparalleled success, the Highlanders/Yankees had never had a pitcher win 300 games. Then along came Phil Niekro.

They called him "Knucksie" because his signature pitch was the knuckleball, and he had used it to baffle hitters for 19 seasons and to win 268 games by January 6, 1984, when the Yankees signed him, at the age of 44, to a two-year, free-agent contract.

Lending his veteran presence to a youthful pitching staff, Niekro led all Yankees pitchers in wins with 16, raising his career total to 284, and in complete games with five, while also pitching the 44th shutout of his career.

As the 1985 season opened, Niekro would have to duplicate his win total of the previous year to become the 18th pitcher in baseball history to win 300 games and the first to do it in a Yankees uniform.

Thirteen days after his 46th birthday, Niekro won his first game of the season, a 2–1 victory over the Cleveland Indians. By August he had won 10 games, and on September 8, he won his 15th game of the season, leaving him one victory away from the magic 300. More important, combined with Ron Guidry, who would win 22 games, Niekro had helped pitch the Yankees into contention in the American League East.

Victory number 300 would prove to be an elusive prize for Niekro, who would lose his next three starts. But with Guidry and Niekro's younger brother, Joe, both winning twice, the Yankees won seven out of eight from September 25 to October 3 to keep their slim championship

hopes alive, three games behind the Blue Jays, as they went to Toronto for the final three games of the season.

The Yankees would have to sweep the Blue Jays just to finish in a tie and force a playoff for the division title, and Phil Niekro was penciled in to pitch the final game of the season.

The Yankees won the opening game of the set on a Friday night, 4–3. But the following day, Doyle Alexander outpitched Joe Cowley, and the Blue Jays clinched the division championship.

The Yankees were eliminated from contention, but there still was incentive on Sunday, October 6, for Niekro. He had been stuck on 299 wins for four weeks as he took the mound for what figured to be his last game in a Yankees uniform.

His teammates came to Niekro's aid early, scoring three runs in the first inning and then adding two more runs in the fifth. Meanwhile, Niekro was disposing of the Blue Jays with dispatch. He held them hitless through the first three innings, then gave up a single to Cecil Fielder in the fourth and a double to Jeff Burroughs in the seventh.

When the Yankees scored two in the top of the eighth, they had opened a commanding 7–0 lead. Niekro could have left the game then and let the Yankees' bullpen, headed by Dave Righetti, finish the game. But he wanted to get the final out of his 300th win himself, and he also had a chance to embellish number 300 with a shutout.

Niekro sailed through the eighth, allowing only a two-out single to Manny Lee. Don Mattingly's fourth hit of the game, and 35th home run of the season, made it 8–0 in the ninth, and Niekro took the mound in the bottom of the ninth, three outs away from win number 300.

He retired Rick Leach on a bouncer back to the mound. One out. Lou Thornton popped to catcher Butch

Wynegar in foul territory. Two outs. But Tony Fernandez, pinch hitting for Fielder, lined a double to center field, putting Niekro's shutout in jeopardy.

The outcome of the game was no longer in doubt, but Niekro wanted the shutout. He faced a former teammate, veteran slugger Burroughs, who had collected one of the four hits allowed by Niekro.

To that point, Niekro, who had lived and flourished with the knuckleball, had not thrown one all game just to prove he could win without his stock in trade.

When he got two strikes on Burroughs, Knucksie threw his only knuckleball of the game. Burroughs swung and missed, and Niekro had become the 18th pitcher in baseball history to win 300 games, and the first to do it wearing a Yankees uniform.

It was Niekro's first shutout of the season, the 45th, and last of his career, and, at the age of 46 years, six months, and five days, he was the oldest man in major league history to pitch a complete-game shutout.

Rocket's Launch

On October 6, 1985, in the Yankees' 85th season in the American League, Phil Niekro became the 18th pitcher in baseball history, and the first Yankee, to win his 300th game.

Exactly 17 years, eight months, and seven days later, Roger Clemens became the 21st pitcher in baseball history, and the second Yankee, to win his 300th game.

Clemens had come to New York a pariah, high on the Yankees' enemies list. As a member of the hated Boston Red Sox for 13 seasons, he was a 20-game winner three times, frequently thwarting Yankees hopes and aspirations. When the Red Sox felt they no longer needed him, Clemens signed as a free agent with the Toronto Blue Jays and tacked on two more 20-win seasons.

But he had outlived his usefulness in Toronto also, and the Blue Jays engineered a trade with the Yankees, sending him to New York on February 18, 1999, in exchange for Homer Bush, Graeme Lloyd, and David Wells.

Clemens arrived in New York with 233 career wins, 3,153 strikeouts, 44 shutouts, and six Cy Young Awards. Although the man they call "the Rocket" was ascending rapidly on baseball's all-time list for pitching prowess and was considered among the greatest pitchers the game has known, Yankees fans did not warmly embrace Clemens's arrival. Old wounds healed slowly for the Yankees faithful, who also lamented the loss of Wells, a fan favorite, who had won 18 games during the 1998 regular season and was a perfect 4–0 in the postseason.

To make matters worse, Wells would win 37 games for the Blue Jays over the next two seasons, and Clemens would win 10 fewer for the Yankees. It wasn't until Clemens pitched a one-hitter against the Mariners and struck out 15 in Game 4 of the 2000 American League Championship Series that New York fans accepted him as a Yankee.

In 2001, Clemens became a full-fledged Yankees idol. He won 20 games, lost only three, and won his seventh Cy Young Award, the first in 23 years by a Yankee.

When the 2003 season started, Clemens was in striking distance of two pitching milestones. He needed seven wins to reach the magic 300 and 91 strikeouts to join Nolan Ryan and Steve Carlton as the only pitchers to record 4,000 Ks.

Clemens won his first four decisions, leaving him two away from 300. On May 21 in Boston's Fenway Park, scene of his greatest triumphs, he bagged number 299, a 4–2 victory over the Red Sox.

As fate would have it, Clemens would go for number 300 five days later at Yankee Stadium, also against the Red Sox, his old team. To witness and commemorate the occasion, Clemens flew members of his family from his Texas home to New York, but it was not to be. He lost to the Red Sox, and the celebration was put on hold until seven days later, when he started against the Reds in Cincinnati.

Again, Clemens was denied, taking a no-decision as the Yankees were beaten, 4–3.

The next stop for the Clemens caravan was Chicago, against the Cubs, on June 7. Matched up with Kerry Wood, another hard-throwing Texan, Clemens lost again, 5–2.

Now it was back to New York for an interleague game against the Cardinals on Friday, the 13th of June. Clemens came out blazing, striking out the side in the first inning, and the Yankees jumped out on top with a run in the bottom of the first on a single by Derek Jeter and a double by Jorge Posada, Clemens's catcher.

The Cardinals tied the score in the second on Jim Edmonds's home run. After Scott Rolen doubled, Clemens fanned Edgar Renteria, his 4,000[th] strikeout. He then struck out Tino Martinez and Mike Matheny, giving him six strike-outs in two innings.

The Yankees regained the lead on Hideki Matsui's home run in the bottom of the second, the Cardinals tied it at 2–2 in the fourth, and the Yankees again regained the lead, 3–2, on Ruben Sierra's home run in the bottom of the fourth.

Clemens held the Cardinals scoreless and nursed his one-run lead through the fifth and sixth innings. In the fifth, after a walk to J.D. Drew and a single by Albert Pujols with one out, Clemens preserved his lead by striking out Edmonds and Rolen, giving him 10 or more strikeouts in a game for the 103rd time in his career.

In the sixth, he retired the side in order, and in the seventh he got the first two batters. He had retired seven straight when manager Joe Torre went to the mound and removed Clemens, who walked off the field to a standing ovation from the Yankee Stadium crowd of 55,214.

Left-hander Chris Hammond was summoned to face J.D. Drew, and Clemens had to endure some anxious moments when Drew bunted for a hit and Pujols singled him to second. The tying run was on second, Clemens faced with still another no-decision, another disappointment, and the dangerous Edmonds coming to bat. But Hammond got Edmonds to bounce to second, and the one-run lead was preserved.

The Yankees gave Clemens some breathing room with Raul Mondesi's two-run homer in the bottom of the seventh to stretch their lead to 5–2.

Pablo Osuna pitched a perfect eighth, and then the incomparable Mariano Rivera came on to set the Cardinals down in order in the ninth. Roger Clemens, age 40 years, 10 months, and nine days, had his 300th win.

Finally, the thrice-delayed celebration could begin.

39. Mantle's Memorial Day

Mickey Mantle hit 536 home runs during the regular season, one for every 15.1 at-bats, and 18 more in the World Series, one for every 12.8 at-bats.

His first home run came in Chicago on May 1, 1951, off Randy Gumpert. His last came in Yankee Stadium on September 20, 1968, off Jim Lonborg of the Boston Red Sox.

In between, he hit some memorable home runs, mammoth shots that were the stuff of legend.

There was the one off Bill Fischer of the Kansas City Royals on May 22, 1963, that came inches from being the only ball ever hit out of Yankee Stadium.

There was the one off Chuck Stobbs of the Washington Senators in Griffith Stadium on April 17, 1953, that was measured at 562 feet. It began the Mantle legend and introduced into the lexicon of baseball the term "tape-measure home run."

There was the one on June 16, 1962, in front of more than 72,000 fans in Cleveland's Municipal Stadium off Gary Bell of the Indians who served up more Mantle home runs than any other pitcher, eight. It came as a pinch-hitter in Mantle's first at-bat after missing a month because of yet another injury.

There was the game-winning home run off Barney Schultz of the Cardinals on October 10, 1964, in Game 3 of the World Series.

There was the one in Detroit's Tiger Stadium on September 19, 1968, off a benevolent Dennis McLain of the Tigers. It was Mantle's 535th homer, and it put him into third place on the all-time home-run list behind Babe Ruth and Willie Mays.

And there was home run number 140 in Yankee Stadium off Pedro Ramos of the Washington Senators on May 30, 1956.

Ramos was one of Mantle's favorite characters, first as an opponent who was constantly challenging Mantle to a foot race, and later as a teammate.

"He was always bragging that he could run faster than me," Mantle said. "He kept challenging me to a race, and one day Casey Stengel said to him, 'All right, you put up $10,000 and we'll put up $10,000, and Mickey will race you, winner take all.'

"Ramos never did come up with the money, and he never bragged about beating me in a foot race again."

Ramos was also an outstanding right-handed pitcher, whose best pitch was what he called "a Cuban palm ball." Others called it a spitball.

On Opening Day of the 1956 season in Washington, when Mantle had hit two tremendous home runs off Camilo Pascual, another Cuban right-hander with the Senators, Ramos was seen waving a towel and mocking his country-man, friend, and teammate as if to say, "He wouldn't hit two balls like that off me."

In a later series between the two teams, a Yankees pitcher hit a Senator with a pitch. In those days, that meant payback. Washington's pitcher was expected to retaliate by hitting the first Yankee up in the next inning. It just happened that Washington's pitcher was Ramos and the first Yankee scheduled to hit in the next inning was Mantle, who knew what was coming. Ramos threw his first pitch, Mantle turned to cushion the blow, and the ball hit him in the middle of his back.

The following day, a contrite Ramos sheepishly approached Mantle at the batting cage.

"Meekee," Ramos said in his Cuban accent. "I no want to heet you. They make me do it."

"That's all right, Pete," Mantle said. "You got to do what they tell you. But the next time you hit me, I'm going to drag a bunt down the first-base line and run right up your back."

The next time they met was in Yankee Stadium on Memorial Day, 1956, Mantle's Triple Crown year. In the fifth inning of the first game of the doubleheader Mantle hit what he said was "the hardest ball I ever hit left-handed." It struck against the 117-foot-high roof in right field above the 370-foot sign, and it was estimated that had it not hit the roof, the ball would have traveled between 550 and 600 feet.

As Mantle rounded third base, running his home run home, his eye caught Pascual in the Senators dugout waving a towel at Ramos just as Ramos had done to him on Opening Day.

The following day, Ramos again approached Mantle at the batting cage.

"Meekee," he said. "I would rather have you run up my back than have you heet a ball like that off me."

40. Slam, Bang

Had he played for any team other than the Yankees, or at any time other than the late '20s and early '30s, Lou Gehrig may have been hailed as the greatest player the game of baseball has known. He would have invited comparisons with Honus Wagner, Ty Cobb, and Babe Ruth. As a home-run hitter, he would have rivaled the Babe himself.

But alongside the mighty, boisterous, blustery, and bombastic Babe, who was bigger than life, Gehrig paled by comparison. He was forced into a subordinate role: John Adams to George Washington, Marc Antony to Julius Caesar, Buzz Aldrin to Neil Armstrong, Larry Doby to Jackie Robinson.

In 1927, when Gehrig hit an amazing 47 home runs, Ruth hit an even more amazing 60.

In 1931, the first time Gehrig led the American League in home runs with 46, he had to share the title with the Babe.

Even in 1932, when Ruth was beginning his decline, he remained an imposing presence not yet ready to transfer the mantle of Yankee leadership to his more unobtrusive teammate. While Gehrig would outhit Ruth by eight points that season, .349 to .341, and drive in 14 more runs, 151 to 137, he still could not surpass Ruth in home runs. Gehrig swatted 35, Ruth 41.

But for one day, Gehrig would stand apart from Ruth and accomplish something that even the Babe never had.

On June 3, 1932, the Yankees faced the Athletics in Philadelphia's Shibe Park. Pitching for the Athletics was George Earnshaw, who had won 68 games in the previous three seasons, plus four World Series victories, and was regarded by many as the best right-hander in the American League.

In the first inning, Gehrig drove a mighty blast over the right-field wall for a home run. In the fourth, he connected again, also over the right-field wall. In the fifth, Gehrig launched his third straight home run over the right-field wall. It was the fourth time in his career Gehrig had hit three home runs in a game.

No other hitter in baseball history, Ruth included, had ever hit three home runs in a game four times, and no hitter in the modern era, not even the mighty Babe, had ever hit four home runs in a game.

In 1894, Bobby Lowe had hit four home runs in a game for the Boston Braves. Two years later, Ed Delahanty hit four home runs for the Philadelphia Phillies. Nobody had done it since in a span of 36 years.

After Gehrig's third home run, Philadelphia manager Connie Mack removed Earnshaw from the game, replaced him with Leroy Mahaffey, and instructed Earnshaw to take a seat alongside Mack on the bench.

"Sit here for a few minutes, son," Mack said. "I want you to see how Mahaffey does it. You've been pitching entirely wrong to Gehrig."

In the seventh inning, Mahaffey threw a fastball, and Gehrig belted it over the left-field wall for his fourth consecutive home run.

"I understand now, Mr. Mack," Earnshaw said. "Mahaffey made Gehrig change his direction. Can I take my shower now?"

Gehrig would get two more chances for a fifth home run as the Yankees pounded out 20 runs and 23 hits. He grounded out in the eighth. In the ninth, he drove a tremendous shot to deep center field. Athletics center fielder Al Simmons took off after the ball and, in full stride, leaped high against the wall and speared the ball just as it was headed over the wall.

"That last ball I hit was the hardest one I hit all day," Gehrig said. "But Simmons caught up with it. How do you figure it?"

As the first hitter to blast four home runs in a game in the 20ᵗʰ century, Gehrig's was a monumental achievement, one worthy of blaring headlines in New York newspapers. And it would have had those headlines on any other day.

On that day, it rained in New York, where the Giants were scheduled to play the Phillies. Reporters assigned to cover the game arrived at the Polo Grounds to learn that the game had been postponed but also that a notice had been posted in the Giants clubhouse. It stated that after 30 years and 10 National League pennants, John McGraw, "the Little Napoleon," had decided to step down as manager of the Giants and turn the job over to first baseman Bill Terry.

That would be the big story in the newspapers of June 4, 1932, Page 1 in the August *New York Times*, and dominant in newspaper and radio accounts all across the nation.

Buried in the sports pages was the amazing feat of Gehrig, who once again was reduced to playing a subordinate role.

10 Not-So-Magical Moments

Workers survey the wreckage of the crash that killed Thurman Munson and
devastated the Yankees and the baseball community.

1. Tears for the Captain

With three straight American League pennants and two World Series titles after a 12-year drought, and with all their major players in place, plus the addition of free agents Tommy John and Luis Tiant, the Yankees were sending signs in 1979 that they were in the midst of still another dynasty, one to parallel their successes of the '30s, '40s, and '50s.

But as they geared up for a fourth consecutive pennant in 1979, the wheels began to fall off the wagon.

The first bolt came loose on April 19. After a slow start, the Yankees had begun to roll. They won the first two games of a three-game series against the Orioles and closed to a half game behind Baltimore. A sweep would move the Yankees into first place in the American League East on their way to what would surely be their fourth straight pennant.

It was hardly cause for alarm or panic when Hall of Famer Jim Palmer beat them, 6–3, to avoid the sweep and keep the Yankees out of first place. What would happen in the Yankees' shower room after the game would have far greater ramifications.

It began with typical ballplayer needling between veteran catcher/designated hitter Cliff Johnson and Goose Gossage, the Yankees' dominant relief pitcher who had led the league with 27 saves and won 10 other games the previous year. Soon the needling escalated, tempers flared, and Johnson and Gossage were scuffling. Johnson shoved Gossage against a wall, and as he began to tumble to the floor, Gossage tried to break his fall with his hands and landed on his right thumb, all 230 pounds of him.

The result was a tear of the ulnar collateral ligament in the joint of the right thumb. Gossage would undergo surgery three days later and would not pitch again until the middle of July.

On June 2, while jogging in from the outfield, Reggie Jackson suffered a partial tear of the sheath of muscle in his left calf area. He would be sidelined for almost a month.

Graig Nettles, the fielding star of the 1978 World Series, was beset with a series of minor injuries that would hamper his hitting and cause his batting average to drop 23 points, his home runs to dip from 27 to 20, and his RBIs to decrease from 93 to 73.

On June 18, with the Yankees struggling with a record of 34–30 and in fourth place, eight games out of first, manager Bob Lemon was fired. To light a spark in the team, Billy Martin was brought back one year earlier than had been planned.

The Yankees played better under Martin. They would win 55 of their last 95 games with Martin as manager, but they were buried too far behind and beset with too many problems to overcome the runaway Orioles.

Not the least of the Yankees' problems was what to do with their captain, their heart and soul, Thurman Munson. Years of squatting behind home plate had taken a toll on Munson's knees, and it was becoming increasingly obvious that his days as a full-time catcher were behind him. He began taking fly balls in the outfield. The plan was to limit Munson's catching duty to about two or three times a week, and on the days when he did not catch to use him as a designated hitter, at first base, or in right field. The thought of Munson not being their full-time catcher was disturbing to his teammates, who relied heavily on his skill, knowledge, and leadership.

"Having him there, everybody kind of revolved around him," said Ron Guidry, the team's pitching ace. "You could take me out, and they could still win. You could take anybody else out, and they would probably still win. But if you took Thurman out, our chances of winning were cut in half."

Not only were Munson's physical problems taking their toll, but he was also agonizing over lengthy absences from his family. A devoted husband and father, Thurman had chosen not to disrupt his children's schooling by moving them to the home in New Jersey he occupied during the season. His wife, Diane, daughters Kelly and Tracy, and son Michael–who needed special care because he was hyperactive–remained back home in Ohio, and Munson knew his place was with them.

To limit the length of the absences, Munson began taking flying lessons after the 1977 season and then purchased a Cessna Citation, his objective being to fly home as often as possible when there was a break in the Yankees' schedule.

Ordinarily, teams frowned on a player flying his own plane, especially during the season. But Munson was special to the Yankees, and they looked the other way to accommodate him.

Asked about his flying, Munson said, "I think it's great, the feeling of being alone for an hour or two. You're up there and nobody asks any questions. You don't have to put on any kind of an act. You just go up there and enjoy yourself. You have to be on your toes, but it's kind of relaxing when you spend a lot of time by yourself, and I need that. I also need to get home a lot, so I love to fly."

On July 26, the Yankees shut out the California Angels, 2–0, behind Guidry's three-hitter, completing their first homestand after the All-Star break with six wins in eight games. It put them 10 games over .500 but still left them in fourth place, 12 games behind Baltimore.

Looking ahead at the Yankees' schedule, Munson noted an upcoming trip that would take them to Milwaukee and Chicago, and that August 2, the day after the final game of a three-game series in Chicago, was a day off in the schedule. Munson made plans to fly his plane to Chicago after the final game of the homestand so the plane would be waiting for him when the series with the White Sox ended. He would then fly from Chicago to Canton and spend the day off with his family before flying back to New York for the start of a homestand against the Orioles on Friday night, August 3.

On July 27, the Yankees lost the series opener in Milwaukee, 6–5. It would be the last game Munson would ever catch. He sat out the second game of the series against the Brewers and played first base in the third game. He then played first base in the opener of the three-game series in Chicago, was the designated hitter in the second game, and started at first base in the series finale, a 9–1 Yankees victory.

In the last game he would ever play, Munson walked in the first inning and scored in front of Jackson's home run. He struck out in the third and then was given the rest of the game off, replaced by Jim Spencer.

After the game, the Yankees flew back to New York by charter, and Munson flew to Canton in his private plane to spend his mini-holiday with his family.

Munson arrived in Canton in time for dinner with his family and planned to rise early the next day to practice takeoffs and landings in his Cessna Citation at Akron-Canton Airport. Coming in for a landing, Munson apparently lost control and the plane crashed 1,000 feet short of the runway. Rescuers got Munson's two flying companions safely out of the plane. Munson was not so fortunate. Rescuers were unable to free him from the burning wreckage.

News of the tragedy spread quickly. Munson's teammates, his friends, were devastated.

Willie Randolph: "It was total shock…stunned. You hear what people are saying to you, but you don't believe it. No, there's no way this happened. I was just with him the other night. We were sitting there joking, playing cards. It was total shock. Disbelief. I broke down and cried."

Chris Chambliss: "Audrey [Mrs. Chambliss] and I were going to get some ice cream, not far from our house in New Jersey. We were driving down the street and the guy on the radio said, 'Thurman Munson just died.' I heard the word 'crash.' And Audrey and I just looked at each other and didn't say a word for I don't know how long. We were just stunned…quiet.… We didn't say anything to each other for a long, long time. We were both so shocked."

Bucky Dent: "The last time I saw Thurman, we played a game in Comiskey Park, and I was sitting on the bus and I saw Thurman and Bobby Murcer and Bobby's wife, Kay, come walking out in front of the bus and then go to their car.

"The next day, the day off, I was out all day, and then I went to the Twin Towers for dinner. After dinner, I was going to get my car and some guy said, 'Aren't you Bucky Dent?'

"I said, 'Yeah,' and he said, 'Isn't it a shame what happened to Thurman?' I said, 'What are you talking about?' He said, 'He got killed in a plane crash.'

"It stunned me. I kind of fell back on the car. I said, 'No, that's not true.' He said it was, and I asked him, 'Was there anybody with him?' and he said, 'Yeah, there were two other people in the plane.'

"My first reaction was I thought it was Bobby Murcer and his wife.

"As it turned out, one of the people in the plane with Thurman was Jerry Anderson, who was my partner in my baseball school. Jerry later told me Thurman was going to do some touch-and-gos, and Thurman asked Jerry, who was a flying instructor, to go up with him. He did, and he brought a buddy with him.

"Thurman was doing some landings on an elevated runway. He was coming in and he put the landing gear down and dropped his air speed, and the plane hit and spun up on top of the road and burst into flames. They kicked out the side door, and Jerry and the other guy got out. Jerry was burned, but he said when the plane hit on Thurman's side, it jammed Thurman up and broke his neck and he couldn't move. That's why he couldn't get out."

Billy Martin was spending his day off fishing somewhere on the Jersey shore. It was the duty of Yankees public relations director Mickey Morabito to locate Martin and give him the terrible news.

"I didn't know where Billy was," said Morabito, "but I had the phone number of the harbormaster, so I called him and told him to get Billy off the boat, it was an emergency.

"I waited a long time and then I heard Billy's voice on the line and I told him the news. At first, he didn't believe me. 'No,' he said. 'It's not true.'

"I convinced him it was by giving him all the details, and Billy started to sob. He was crying like a baby. Billy was such an emotional guy, and he loved Thurman. I don't remember Billy saying good-bye. He ended the conversation by just hanging up the phone without a word, that's how broken up he was."

The funeral was held on August 6 in Canton, a Monday afternoon. George Steinbrenner arranged a charter plane to fly the players, their wives, manager, coaches, executives, trainers, clubhouse attendants, front-office workers, and members of the press from Newark Airport to Canton.

Players and former players, former teammates and opponents, umpires and baseball executives came from all over the country to say their last good-byes to a player who was universally respected for his competitiveness and his desire to win.

The flight back to New York was solemn, the entire day had been emotionally draining and wrenching, but there was a game to play that night. First, there was a pregame memorial to the Yankees' fallen captain.

The Yankees took the field, and the area behind home plate, Thurman Munson's customary position, was left vacant during the ceremony. Munson's image flashed on the huge message board in right center field, superimposed by these words:

Our captain and leader has not left us–today, tomorrow, this year, next…our endeavors will reflect our love and admiration for him.

Yankees stood at their respective positions, hats removed, heads bowed. In right field, Jackson, with whom Munson had feuded for almost two seasons, brushed tears from his eyes.

Terence Cardinal Cooke of New York led the assembled fans in prayer. The crowd of 36,314 stood in silence during the ceremony, and then, as one, they began to applaud and chant Munson's name.

121

The Orioles raced to an early 4–0 lead. In the seventh inning, Murcer, who had been one of the eulogists at the funeral just hours before, belted a three-run home run to cut Baltimore's lead to 4–3.

In the bottom of the ninth, Murcer batted again, this time with the bases loaded. He lashed a single that drove in two runs and gave the Yankees a dramatic, come-from-behind 5–4 victory. After the game, Murcer didn't have to say a word. Everybody knew he won the game for his buddy, Thurman.

A-maz-ing

In his first 10 years as manager of the Yankees, Casey Stengel had won nine American League pennants and seven World Series. But in his 11th season at their helm, the team had plummeted uncharacteristically.

The 1959 Yankees had won only 79 games, 13 fewer than the previous year, and finished in third place, 15 games behind the Chicago White Sox.

Was this the end of a dynasty?

Had Stengel, nearing his 71st birthday, lost his magic?

In an effort to repair the damage, the Yankees made several key moves for the 1960 season. Clete Boyer, obtained from Kansas City the previous year, took over at third base, replacing Hector Lopez, a good hitter but poor fielder who was switched to the outfield. Elston Howard became the everyday catcher, replacing an aging Yogi Berra.

The big move, however, was a seven-player trade with the Athletics on December 11, 1959, that sent longtime Yankees star Hank Bauer and Don "Perfect Game" Larsen to Kansas City in exchange for a young, left-handed power hitter named Roger Maris.

In his first season as a Yankee, Maris would bat .283, drive in a league-leading 112 runs, blast 39 home runs (one behind teammate Mickey Mantle for the league lead), be voted American League Most Valuable Player, and help the Yankees win 97 games, 18 more than the previous season, and another pennant by eight games over the Baltimore Orioles.

In the National League, a new power had emerged. Assembled by master builder Branch Rickey, the Pittsburgh Pirates, with veterans Dick Stuart, Dick Groat, Bill Mazeroski, Bill Virdon, Bob Skinner, and Smoky Burgess, 20-game winner Vernon Law, and a rising star, Roberto Clemente, finished seven games ahead of the Milwaukee Braves and won their first pennant in 33 years.

The 1960 World Series would be a rematch of the 1927 classic, but while the '27 Yankees of Babe Ruth and Lou Gehrig, considered by many the greatest team in baseball history, disposed of the overmatched Pirates in four games, the 1960 World Series was thought to be a toss-up.

With the first two games of the Series to be played in Pittsburgh's Forbes Field, with its short left field known as Kiner's Korner, and the Pirates stocked with an array of powerful right-handed hitters, Stengel opted to open with his two best right-handed pitchers and save left-hander Whitey Ford for Game 3 in Yankee Stadium, with its cavernous expanse in left field and left center.

Art Ditmar, who had led the Yankees with 15 victories, got the ball for Game 1. It was a mistake. Ditmar failed to get out of the first inning as the Pirates scored three runs on a walk, a double, two singles, and two stolen bases before Jim Coates could replace him and end the damage.

The Pirates added two runs in the fourth on a two-run home run by Mazeroski, a sign of things to come, and another run in the sixth as Law pitched out of trouble in every inning, limiting the Yankees to two runs despite allowing 10 hits over seven innings. A two-run pinch-hit home run by Howard in the ninth made the final score Pittsburgh 6, New York 4.

To start the second game, Stengel chose Bob Turley, another right-hander. The Yankees made his task easy by pounding out 19 hits. Mantle blasted two home runs and drove in five runs in a 16–3 rout.

With the Series tied, one game each, the scene moved to Yankee Stadium for Game 3, and Stengel's decision to hold Ford out of the first two games was vindicated. Ford was brilliant in limiting the Pirates to four hits. The Yankees erupted for six runs in the first, the big blow a grand slam by Bobby Richardson. The Yankees collected 16 hits, four by Mantle, who belted his third homer of the Series, and won another rout, this time by the score of 10–0.

The Pirates evened the Series with a 3–2 victory in Game 4 as Law outpitched Ralph Terry.

Ditmar got his second start in Game 5 and again was knocked out early, this time in the second inning. Harvey Haddix and El Roy Face combined to hold the Yankees to five hits in a 5–2 victory that gave the Pirates a 3–2 lead in games and sent them back to Pittsburgh needing one victory in two games to reign as world champions for the first time in 35 years.

But they had to face Ford in Game 6. Once again, the Yankees' left-hander was brilliant. Pitching on three days' rest, Ford delivered his second straight shutout, a seven-hitter, and the Yankees rattled 17 more hits around Forbes Field in a 12–0 rout.

Two straight shutouts and holding the Pirates scoreless in Forbes Field were little consolation for Ford, still smarting over Stengel's decision to save him for Game 3 in Yankee Stadium rather than pitch him in the Series opening game in Pittsburgh.

"I felt I should have started the first game of the Series," Ford said, "but Stengel had this thing about saving me for Yankee Stadium to take advantage of the big left field and left center, Death Valley to right-handed hitters. The way I figured it, either way I was going to have to pitch at least one game in Pittsburgh. Why not two?

"It gets late early out there."
—Yogi Berra, on playing left field during day games in the World Series when shadows fall quickly

---

"I had missed the first six weeks of the season because of a bad shoulder. I didn't pitch well in the first half, but I finished strong [10 wins in his last 14 decisions for a record of 12–9] and I was sure Casey would start me in the first game of the World Series, which would have given me a chance to start three games, if necessary. But Casey had other ideas, and that really ticked me off. It was the only time I ever got mad at Stengel."

With Ford reduced to the role of spectator, Stengel's Game 7 starter was Turley, the winner of Game 2. But the Pirates knocked him out in the second inning and took a 4–0 lead behind Law, looking for his third win of the Series.

Law pitched four shutout innings before the Yankees broke through with a run in the fifth and then knocked Law out by scoring four in the sixth, highlighted by Berra's three-run homer. Two more runs in the eighth gave the Yankees a 7–4 lead, six outs away from another World Series championship.

In the bottom of the eighth, it was the Pirates' turn to rally, aided by a huge break. After Gino Cimoli led off with a pinch-hit single, Virdon hit a perfect double-play ball to shortstop, but the ball hit a pebble, bounced up, and struck Tony Kubek in the Adam's apple. Virdon reached safely and Kubek was removed from the game. When backup catcher Hal Smith hit a three-run homer off Coates, the Pirates had a five-run inning and a 9–7 lead going into the top of the ninth.

The Yankees had one more rally left in their bats. They scored two runs in the top of the ninth to tie the score at 9–9.

The first batter in the bottom of the ninth was Mazeroski. Known mainly for his defense, Maz was considered the best-fielding second baseman in the game. He had hit only 11 homers and had driven in 64 runs during the regular season and had enjoyed a productive Series to that point with a home run and four RBIs.

On the mound for the Yankees was Terry, who had relieved Coates to get the final out in the eighth.

Maz swung at Terry's second pitch and sent it over the head of Berra, playing left field for the Yankees, over the ivy-covered left-field wall, and into the seats. Bedlam erupted in Forbes Field as Mazeroski rounded the bases for the first World Series–winning home run in history.

Sadly, the Yankees trudged off the field, heartbroken losers.

Bill Mazeroski hits a home run that destroys the Yankees' hopes for victory in the 1960 World Series.

> **"I'll never make the mistake of being 70 again."** —Casey Stengel, at the press conference in 1960 in which the Yankees announced his "retirement" as manager

"I never felt so bad in my life," Mantle said. "We were clearly the much better team. The scores of the game prove that. I cried all the way home on the plane from Pittsburgh to New York. It was the only time in my professional career that I cried after losing a game."

"The way I was pitching," said Ford, "I know I would have beaten the Pirates three times and we would have been world champs again. That's why I was so mad with Casey for not starting me in the first game."

For the Series, the Yankees batted .338 as a team to the Pirates' .256, outhit the Pirates 91–60, outscored them 55–27, and out-homered them 10–4. Howard batted .462. Mantle batted .400, hit three home runs, and drove in nine. And Richardson batted .367 and set a World Series record by driving in 12 runs.

The Yankees, to a man, were convinced that this time, the better team did not win.

Stengel would never manage another game for the Yankees. Four days after Mazeroski's historic blast, the Yankees called a press conference to announce that Stengel was retiring.

Someone asked Stengel if he was fired.

"Resigned, fired, quit, discharged, use whatever you damn please," Stengel replied. "I don't care. You don't see me crying about it. I commenced winning pennants when I came here, but I didn't commence getting any younger."

3. Reversing the Curse

The outcome, like death and taxes, was inevitable. Whenever the Yankees opposed their archrivals, the Boston Red Sox, in a critical, winner-take-all situation, with all the chips on the table, the result was always the same. The Yankees prevailed.

It had been so since 1918, when the Red Sox, powered by a young, left-handed pitcher named George Herman "Babe" Ruth, beat the Chicago Cubs in the World Series, four games to two.

Two seasons later, Ruth was sold to the Yankees, thereby shifting the balance of power in the American League for almost a century. Eighty-six years had passed, and the Red Sox had not won another World Series, a drought that would come to be known infamously in Red Sox Nation as "the Curse of the Bambino."

In those 86 years, the Yankees would win 39 American League pennants and 26 World Series; the Red Sox would win four pennants and no World Series.

By 2004, hostilities and enmity between the two teams, and their fans, were at an all-time high. To the Red Sox, the Yankees were "the Evil Empire" and Yankees owner George Steinbrenner was Darth Vader.

For the seventh straight year, the Yankees had finished first in the American League East, and for the seventh straight year, the Red Sox had finished second but they made the playoffs as the American League wild card. When the Yankees defeated the Twins and the Red Sox eliminated the Angels in the division series, these longtime rivals faced off in the American League Championship Series.

The Yankees won the first two games at Yankee Stadium, and when they demolished the Red Sox in front of their own fans in Fenway Park in Game 3 by the lopsided and humiliating score of 19–8, the inevitable was once again at hand.

Adding to the Red Sox's sorry plight was baseball history. No team had ever lost the first three games and come back to win a best-of-seven series.

On October 17, in Boston, the Yankees moved in for the kill. The Red Sox hoped only to avoid the further ignominy of a four-game sweep. But when the Yankees scored two in the sixth to take a 4–3 lead, and the Red Sox failed to score in the sixth, seventh, and eighth, the Yankees were only three outs away from another pennant. In the game to close the deal was their incomparable reliever, Mariano Rivera, who had saved 53 games during the regular season and two more in this series.

A ray of hope dawned on Red Sox Nation when Kevin Millar worked a leadoff walk against the normally impeccable Rivera. Dave Roberts was sent in to run for Millar and in a daring maneuver, Roberts took off for second and stole the base. When Bill Mueller followed with a single, Roberts raced home, and the Red Sox had tied the score against Rivera, the consummate big-game closer.

The game remained tied through the tenth inning and the eleventh. The clock had spun past midnight, the game nearing the five-hour mark when the Red Sox batted in the bottom of the twelfth with veteran Paul Quantrill on the mound for the Yankees.

Manny Ramirez led off with a single, and then David Ortiz launched one high and far into the seats to give the Red Sox a 6–4 victory. The Red Sox had dodged a bullet and lived to play another day.

Game 5, the following night, was another nail-biting marathon and another miracle comeback for the Red Sox. Trailing 4–2, the Sox inched closer on another home run by Ortiz, leading off the bottom of the eighth against Tom Gordon. Millar followed with a walk, again, and Roberts ran for him, again. After Trot Nixon singled, sending Roberts to

The Red Sox lost the first three games of the 2004 ALCS, only to come back and win the last four games against the Yankees.

third, Rivera again came in to pitch. For the second straight night, Rivera blew the save when Jason Varitek lifted a sacrifice fly. And the game went on.

It remained tied deep into the night and into the next morning, through the ninth inning, the tenth, the eleventh, the twelfth, and the thirteenth. In the bottom of the fourteenth, Johnny Damon walked with one out and Ramirez walked with two out. That brought up the redoubtable Ortiz, the man known to his teammates and Red Sox fans as "Big Papi." This time he ripped a single to right off Esteban Loiza, scoring Damon with the winning run, and the Red Sox had a 5–4 victory in the longest postseason game by time in baseball history, five hours and 49 minutes. They also had the consolation of knowing the Yankees were not going to celebrate winning another pennant on Boston turf.

The series shifted back to Yankee Stadium for Game 6 and, if necessary, Game 7, with the Yankees confident they would win one of the final two games and vanquish the Red Sox once more.

On center stage in Game 6 was Curt Schilling, the Red Sox right-hander who had missed most of the season because of ankle surgery. He had started Game 1 of the ALCS and had been tagged for six runs in three innings. Now he was attempting to pitch again seven days later.

With blood oozing from his ankle onto his sock, Schilling was magnificent in Game 6. Aided by Mark Bellhorn's three-run home run in a four-run fourth, Schilling and the Red Sox took a 4–1 lead into the bottom of the eighth. The Yankees pushed across a run in the eighth, and put two runners on with two outs in the bottom of the ninth. But Keith Foulke struck out Tony Clark, the potential winning run, to give the Red Sox a 4–2 win. They were the first team in baseball history to tie a seven-game postseason series after losing the first three games.

The sudden-death seventh game came on October 20 in Yankee Stadium, and the Red Sox wasted little time settling the issue. In the first inning, that man Ortiz did it again, a two-run home run off Kevin Brown, his third homer and 10th and 11th RBIs in the series. In the second inning, Damon blasted a grand slam into the upper deck in right field for a 6–0 lead that stunned the Yankee Stadium crowd of 56,129 into shocked silence.

The rest was anticlimactic as the Red Sox rolled to a 10–3 victory and their first pennant in 18 years.

Not only had the Red Sox deprived the Yankees of their 40th pennant and reversed the 86-year "Curse of the Bambino," they had inflicted upon the Yankees the worst collapse in the history of postseason baseball.

Duel in the Dugout

Reggie Jackson didn't come to the Yankees to become a star; he brought his star with him—47 home runs in his second major league season at the age of 23, two American League home-run championships, Most Valuable Player in 1973, 254 home runs before the age of 30.

But his reception by the Yankees was not what he hoped for or expected.

In New York, he encountered indifference, even resentment, from his manager and teammates. Billy Martin made his dislike of Jackson obvious early on by refusing to pamper and cater to him and bat him in the coveted and prestigious cleanup position.

For his part, Jackson contributed to the unpleasantness by posturing and distancing himself from the rest of the Yankees. The ultimate schism between Jackson and the rest of the Yankees came with his infamous "I'm the straw that stirs the drink" comment in an article in *Sport* magazine.

By mid-June of 1977, Jackson's first season in New York, controversy was the order of the day around the Yankees, a daily soap opera nicknamed the "Bronx Zoo." Distractions came almost every day: George Steinbrenner and Martin, Martin and Jackson, Jackson and Steinbrenner.

The big explosion came on Saturday afternoon, June 18, in Boston as full-scale war broke out in Fenway Park. All the tension, all the turmoil, all the festering hostility erupted in an ugly scene in the visitors' dugout in full view of some 35,000 fans and a national television audience, including Steinbrenner, watching the game at his Tampa home.

It came in the sixth inning of a 10–4 defeat to the Red Sox that dropped the Yankees into third place in the American League East, which only added to the mounting frustration and frayed tempers. Jackson was slow retrieving a double by Jim Rice that landed in the right-field corner. Jackson said it was caution. Martin said it was indifference.

There was a break in the action while Martin walked to the mound to make a pitching change. At the same time, Paul Blair was trotting out to right field. Jackson had taken advantage of the lull to stroll to the fence in front of the Yankees bullpen and was chatting with teammate Fran Healy when he heard footsteps behind him. He turned to see Blair heading his way.

"You here for me?" asked Jackson.

Blair nodded.

"What the hell's going on?" said Jackson.

"You've got to ask Billy that," Blair replied.

A perplexed, astonished, and embarrassed Jackson proceeded to trot toward the Yankees dugout on the third-base side and ducked into the far corner. Martin was at the opposite end, closest to home plate, but he headed toward the end of the dugout where Jackson was.

There were words between them, and then Martin, red-faced, the veins bulging in his neck, was attempting to get at Jackson and being restrained in a bear hug by coach Yogi Berra.

This is Jackson's version of the incident from his autobiography, *Reggie*:

When I got to the top step of the dugout, I could see there was a fury about him [Martin], and it was all directed toward me. When Billy starts to lose it, the veins in his neck become more prominent. Now they were standing at attention.

I started down the steps toward the other corner of the dugout from where he was. He screamed over to me.

"What the [bleep] do you think you're doing out there?"

I put my glove down and took my glasses off. I put the glasses down on the top of my glove. Afterward, everybody read that as a sign that I was getting myself ready to fight him. I wasn't. At the time, I was just taking my glasses off, which I often do when I come off the field.

I looked at him.

I said, "What do you mean? What are you talking about?"

He started down the dugout toward me.

"You know what the [bleep] I'm talking about," he said. "You want to show me up by loafing on me? Fine. Then I'm going to show your ass up. Anyone who doesn't hustle doesn't play for me."

"I wasn't loafing, Billy," I said. "But I'm sure that doesn't matter to you. Nothing I could ever do would please you. You never wanted me on this team in the first place. You don't want me now. Why don't you just admit it?"

The distance between us had shortened considerably. Elston Howard was trying to get between us. Yogi was there, and Jimmy Wynn.

Billy was still screaming.

"I ought to kick your [bleeping] ass," was the next thing I heard. And then I'd had enough.

"Who the [bleep] do you think you're talking to, old man?" I snapped, just about spitting out the words.

"What?" Billy yelled. "Who's an old man? Who are you calling an old man?"

I guess in Billy's mind he was still 25 years old and the toughest kid on the street corner. He came for me. Elston and Yogi grabbed him. Jimmy Wynn grabbed me from behind.

"You're an old man," I said. "You're 49 years old and you weigh 160. I'm 30 and weigh 210. Let me tell you something: You aren't going to do [bleep]. What you are is plain crazy."

This was Martin's version:

I didn't like the way Reggie went after the ball. I thought he dogged it, and I just can't have that sort of thing on my team. I had told my players at the beginning of the season if they embarrassed me on the field, I was going to embarrass them. I knew the other 24 players were looking to see how I was going to handle this, with Reggie being a superstar and having the big contract. I thought if I did what had to be done, that would bring George down on me. But if I let it pass, I would lose the other 24 players.

I knew what I had to do. I told Paul Blair to go out to right field and tell Reggie he was being replaced. I meant to teach him a lesson.

When he came into the dugout, Reggie challenged me. He kept telling me he didn't like being shown up, and I replied, "If you show me up, I'll show you up." Then he swore at me, and that did it, we almost came to blows. Elston Howard and Yogi Berra had to pull us apart.

Jackson left the stadium and returned to the team's hotel. Several hours later, he was visited in his room by three reporters.

Mike Torrez, the Yankees' starting pitcher that afternoon, was in Jackson's room to console his friend. Jackson appeared to be near a breakdown. He was stripped to the waist, medals and chains around his neck, dangling at his chest. Perspiration glistened on his bare chest, and soon tears began to stream down his face.

He was on his knees, as if in prayer, delivering a sermon like an evangelist, pouring out anger, frustration, and anguish along with his perspiration and tears, wondering why he was persecuted, why he was so misunderstood, unappreciated, and unwanted. The sweat and the tears formed a pool on the floor at his knees.

"It makes me cry the way they treat me on this team," he said. "I'm a big, black man with an IQ of 160, making $700,000 a year, and they treat me like dirt. They never had anyone like me on their team before."

5. Copa Cutups

It was Billy Martin's birthday, an occasion that called for a celebration–although those Yankees of the 1950s never needed an official occasion to party.

The 29th birthday of Alfred Manuel Martin fell on May 16, 1957, a Thursday, not a good day for a party, especially with a game scheduled the following afternoon. But that Sunday, May 19, was an afternoon game against Cleveland, and there was no game scheduled for Monday, May 20.

Perfect! The celebration would be put on hold for three days. It would take place on Sunday, May 19.

The organizers were Mickey Mantle and Whitey Ford, Martin's two closest buddies on the team. After the game, they would meet up with their wives, and with teammates Yogi Berra, Hank Bauer, Johnny Kucks, and their wives–Martin, unmarried at the time, would go stag. They would all go for dinner at a midtown Manhattan bistro called Danny's Hideaway, a favorite among athletes, actors, and politicians in the day.

When dinner was over, the night was still young. What to do with the remainder of the evening?

The restaurant's proprietor, Danny Stradella, had a suggestion and a generous offer. He had a reserved table at the famous nightclub the Copacabana, where Sammy Davis Jr. was the headline performer at the time. The group was welcome to use Stradella's table. They gratefully accepted the offer and all 11 in the party headed for the Copa.

What happened next is hazy and open to speculation. Here is one eyewitness version from Whitey Ford:

> There was another group sitting not too far from us at a big, long table. It turned out it was a bowling team, and they had been there several hours. That was obvious because they were pretty well juiced, and they were making a lot of noise. They started calling Sammy Davis "Sambo" and making other racial remarks like that.

> Bauer yelled over to them to cool it, in a nice way, not hostile. The next thing we knew, one of the guys said, "Who's going to make me?"

> Then he got up and it looked like he and Bauer were going to get into it. They walked to a room in the back and the rest of us got up and followed, just in case.

> The guy who said that to Hank got to the back room before any of us, even Hank. All of a sudden, we heard a crash, and by the time we got there, the guy was stretched out on the floor. My eyes never left Hank, so I know he didn't do it. And Billy was right next to me all the time, so I know he didn't do it. To this day, I don't know who slugged the guy. I think it was one of the Copa bouncers because it was a real professional job.

> I knew one thing: we had to get out of there fast. If it hit the papers, we'd be in deep trouble. One of the bouncers must have realized the same thing because he led us out of the place through an exit in the rear. Joan [Ford's wife] said she never knew what happened, just that she and the other wives were being ushered out of the Copa through the kitchen and into the lobby of a hotel next to the nightclub. When we had assembled in the hotel lobby, we all went to our cars and went home.

The partygoers' fears were realized the next morning when they saw the headlines in the New York newspapers: "Yankees in Copa Fight." The six Yankees were summoned to the office of the team's general manager, George Weiss, who was so angry he fined each player $1,000.

"Naturally, Weiss was steaming," said Martin. "Just as naturally, he blamed me. I didn't hit the guy. I was nowhere near him, but I got blamed. When I told

Weiss my side of the story, he didn't believe me. He never liked me and he was trying to get rid of me anyway, but Casey [Stengel] wouldn't let him. Now, Weiss had an excuse. I knew I was gone. I even told Mickey and Whitey so."

The following day, Yankees owner Dan Topping brought in his lawyer to meet with the six players who were being sued for damages by the members of the bowling team.

"The lawyer asked us to tell him exactly what happened, and we did," said Ford. "And he said, 'Fine, tell that story to the grand jury just like you told it to me.' And that was it. We were with the lawyer less than an hour, and all he told us to do was tell the grand jury the same story we told him, and then the guy sent us a bill for $6,500. So, between the fine and the lawyer's fee, it cost us more than $2,000 apiece for doing nothing. The grand jury even threw the case out.

"At the grand jury hearing, Mantle was standing in the middle of the room, giving his testimony. There was no chair, nothing. He was standing there chewing gum, and the judge asked him, 'What are you chewing, Mr. Mantle?'

"'Gum,' Mick said.

"'Would you mind taking it out of your mouth?'

"Mickey took the gum out of his mouth and there was no place to put it, so he had to hold it in his hand for the rest of the time he was being questioned."

It took almost a month, but Martin's prediction that Weiss would use the Copa incident to get rid of him came true. On June 15, the Yankees traded Martin, Ralph Terry, Woodie Held, and Bob Martyn to Kansas City in exchange for Ryne Duren, Jim Pisoni, and Harry Simpson.

"I cried when Casey called me into his office and told me I was traded," said Martin. "Mickey came over to me and he was crying. Whitey started crying.

"I didn't sleep a wink that night. Mickey, Whitey, and I stayed out all night, and most of the time we were in tears.

"We happened to be in Kansas City at the time and that made it strange because the next day I went to the ballpark and had to move from one clubhouse to the other after all those years. One day I'm playing for the Yankees, and the next day I'm playing against them. Johnny Kucks was pitching, and the first time up I hit a shot off the left-field wall. In the seventh inning, with a man on, I hit a home run that put the Athletics ahead. As I circled the bases, I was in a daze. I felt like a traitor.

"Taking off the pinstripes and going to a second-division team hurt a lot. In my heart, I was a Yankee and I always would be a Yankee."

From left to right: Mickey Mantle, ex-teammate Billy Martin, and Hank Bauer with his wife. The three men appeared before a grand jury that returned a "no bill" on the charge that Bauer beat a New York delicatessen owner in the Copacabana nightclub during Martin's birthday party.

6. Take My Wife, Please!

A new era dawned for the Yankees with the start of the 1973 season.

George Steinbrenner took over as the team's managing general partner, determined to return the Yankees to their championship glory years, and there were two trades of note that would have a significant impact on the team's fortunes.

The first trade came on November 27, 1972, some six weeks before Steinbrenner was introduced as the Yankees' new owner. In exchange for four young players, John Ellis, Jerry Kenney, Charlie Spikes, and Rusty Torres, the Yankees obtained from the Cleveland Indians Graig Nettles, a player that manager Ralph Houk had coveted for several years because of his solid defensive play at third base and his left-handed power stroke that was tailor-made for Yankee Stadium's short right-field fence.

Nettles would become a fixture at third base for the Yankees for more than a decade. His glove work would invite favorable comparisons to Baltimore's Brooks Robinson, and his potent bat would produce 250 home runs in his 11 seasons in New York.

The other trade was so bizarre it defied belief.

Fritz Peterson and Mike Kekich were a pair of left-handed pitchers, blithe spirits, fun-loving, and somewhat eccentric.

Peterson had come up through the Yankees' farm system, joining the big club to stay in 1966, when he showed great potential by winning 12 games as a rookie. Four years later, he won 20 games, and going into the 1973 season, he had won 101 games in seven seasons.

Kekich was obtained in a trade with the Dodgers in 1969. A hard thrower and deep thinker, he had finally shown some promise by winning 10 games each in the 1971 and 1972 seasons and was counted on to take a regular spot in the Yankees' starting rotation in '73.

When Kekich arrived in New York, he hit it off with Peterson almost immediately. The two became close friends, practically inseparable. They were together constantly during the season, and in the off-season they and their wives even vacationed together.

"They were always together," said teammate Gene Michael. "If one of them was walking through the lobby of our hotel on the road, he would be asking where the other one was. That's how close they were."

When spring training '73 opened for the Yankees in Fort Lauderdale on Florida's east coast, Peterson was a no-show. He was on Florida's west coast, holding out in a contract dispute.

A few days into spring training, Yankees president Mike Burke and general manager Lee MacPhail summoned the writers covering the team to manager Houk's office for an announcement, the sort of meeting that normally produced major news, like a blockbuster trade.

The story was a major one, all right, and it was a blockbuster trade, but not the conventional kind.

The door to Houk's office was closed, and MacPhail proceeded to sheepishly and haltingly relate a story that stunned the assembled media. Peterson and Kekich, MacPhail revealed, had entered into an arrangement whereby they would trade wives. Not just wives, but children, family pets, and residences. Peterson would move in with Kekich's wife and children in the Kekich home; Kekich would move in with Peterson's wife and children in the Peterson home. Their intention, agreed to by their wives, was for each player to obtain a divorce and marry the other's spouse.

"I didn't believe it when I first heard about it because it was Peterson and Kekich," said Gene Michael. "These two guys were always pulling some stunt. They were big practical jokers, especially Peterson. He would order things out of a catalog, like fishing gear and hunting rifles, and have them sent to Thurman Munson at Yankee Stadium. Thurman would get these packages, and he had no idea how they got there. And Fritz would be hiding around the corner watching Thurman opening the packages, and Fritz would be laughing like crazy.

"So when my wife told me she heard they were swapping wives, I said, 'Don't believe that stuff. Those guys are pulling some trick again.' That's the first thing I thought because they were always doing some crazy thing, one after another. It never ended."

Some Yankees, including Houk, had heard about the planned swap months before.

"We were in Milwaukee, and Peterson asked me if he could go back to New York early," said Houk. "Peterson's wife had been with him in Milwaukee, but he needed to return to New York and Kekich would drive Fritz's wife home. I saw nothing wrong with that, so I gave him permission.

"It was soon after that that I heard about their plans to swap wives. I talked to both of them, and they were very happy with their arrangement, so what are you going to say? In all my years in baseball, that was the biggest surprise that ever happened to me."

Two months into the season, Kekich was traded to the Indians. He would win only seven more games in the major leagues, and by 1977, he would be out of baseball. He enrolled in medical school and became a doctor. He and the former Marilyn Peterson never married, and they split soon after the swap was revealed.

Not surprisingly, Peterson slipped from 17 wins in 1972 to eight in 1973. The following year, he, too, was traded to Cleveland. He would win only 24 more games for the Indians and Texas Rangers before getting his release from Texas following the 1976 season.

A quarter of a century after the wife swapping, Peterson was still married to the former Susan Kekich.

7. Bummer!

This, members of the Brooklyn Dodgers and their fans believed, truly believed, was next year.

Hadn't they said that before? Hadn't "Wait 'til Next Year" been the rallying cry for the past 10 years of the team known as "Brooklyn's Beloved Bums"?

In that time, they had won four National League pennants, in 1947, '49, '52, and '53, and each time they met up with, and were beaten by, their intracity rival, the New York Yankees.

In 1947, they had been handcuffed in Game 7 by reliever Joe Page, who allowed just one hit over the final five innings.

In 1949, they were blown away in five games.

In 1952, they were done in by Billy Martin's game-saving catch with the bases loaded in the seventh inning of Game 7.

In 1953, it was Martin again, who batted .500, hit two home runs, and drove in eight. The Yankees won in six games against a Dodgers team that had won 105 games, led the major leagues in batting, runs scored, and home runs, and was considered the best ever to represent the borough of Brooklyn.

Now it was 1955 and the Dodgers were back in the World Series, their hopes soaring once more. This was "next year."

The Dodgers had won their first 10 games, 22 of their first 24, and rolled to the National League pennant by 13½ games over the Milwaukee Braves. Again, they had led the majors in batting, runs scored, and home runs.

They were essentially the same team as 1953, a little older, but still potent with Duke Snider, who led the league in RBIs and also belted 42 home runs; Gil Hodges, who drove in 102 runs; and Roy Campanella, who knocked in 107, hit 32 home runs, and won his third Most Valuable Player award. Big Don Newcombe headed a strong pitching staff with a spectacular 20–5 record.

After a one-year absence, the Yankees had also returned to the World Series, led by Mickey Mantle, the American League home-run leader with 37; Yogi Berra, who, like Campanella, would win his third Most Valuable Player award; and 18-game winner Whitey Ford.

Yankees versus Dodgers was becoming an annual October affair, and always the outcome was the same. This time would be different, the Dodgers vowed.

But it wasn't different, at least not in the first two games, played in Yankee Stadium. The Yankees knocked Newcombe out in the sixth inning and beat the Dodgers in Game 1, 6–5. Newcombe had started three World Series games against the Yankees and lost all three. In Game 2, Tommy Byrne did what no National League left-hander had been able to do all season: pitch a complete-game victory over the Dodgers. The score was 4–2.

There was gloom in Brooklyn as the Series shifted to Ebbets Field for the next three games. No team had ever won the World Series after losing the first two games, and the Dodgers had never won a World Series in seven tries, five of them against the Yankees.

To start the critical third game, Dodgers manager Walter Alston chose Johnny Podres, a brash left-hander who had won only nine games during the regular season. He would be pitching against the Yankees on his 23rd birthday, and on his young shoulders would rest the Dodgers' sagging hopes.

"After we lost the second game, it was like, 'Oh, no, here we go again,' said Podres. "But I beat them in the third game, and Jackie Robinson told me, 'That's the most important game you ever pitched.'"

In Game 4, the Dodgers bashed four homers, two by Snider, and one each by Campanella and Hodges, to

Dodgers left fielder Sandy Amoros makes a catch against the Yankees in the 1955 World Series.

even the Series at two games apiece by outslugging the Yankees, 8–5.

Snider hit two more home runs in Game 5, and the Dodgers won again, 5–3. Brooklyn's hopes soared once more as the Dodgers took a three-games-to-two lead in the Series.

The home team had won all five games played, which did not bode well for Brooklyn with the last two games to be played in Yankee Stadium. Alston had already told Podres he would be the Dodgers' starting pitcher in Game 7, if there was a Game 7, bypassing 20-game winner Newcombe and veteran Carl Erskine.

"Alston felt he needed a left-hander in Yankee Stadium, and I was the guy," Podres said. "Newcombe couldn't get them out. Erskine couldn't get them out. Who was he going to pitch? Karl Spooner started the sixth game, and [Moose] Skowron hit a three-run homer in the first. Whitey Ford pitched a four-hitter in the sixth game and beat us, 5–1, so that meant I would be pitching in the seventh game. Now every time I see Ford I say, 'Thanks, Whitey. You gave me a shot to be the MVP of the Series.'"

With youthful bravado, Podres put on his customary cocky pose. After the sixth game, he told Dodgers captain Pee Wee Reese, "Don't worry, Pee Wee, I'll shut them out tomorrow."

Next day, on the bus carrying the Dodgers from Brooklyn to Yankee Stadium, Podres boldly told his older, more experienced teammates, four of whom would be elected to the Hall of Fame, "Just get me one run today. That's all I need. Just one."

True to his boast, Podres breezed through the early innings, allowing just three hits but no runs for five innings. The Dodgers had given him the one run he requested in the fourth, and just for good measure, added a run in the sixth.

With a 2–0 lead, Alston made two critical defensive changes as the Yankees came to bat in the bottom of the sixth. Jim Gilliam, who started the game in left field, was brought in to play second base, his regular position, in place of Don Zimmer. To play left field, Alston sent in

Sandy Amoros, a speedy Cuban. The moves would pay almost immediate dividends.

Martin led off the bottom of the sixth with a walk and Gil McDougald beat out a bunt, giving the Yankees their first serious threat of the game, runners on first and second, nobody out, and Berra coming to bat.

Berra sliced a high, twisting fly ball toward the left-field corner that looked like it would land inside the foul line and score both runners. This is where Alston's defensive changes paid off. Amoros was shaded toward center field against Berra, a dead-pull hitter, but he was off at the crack of the bat and with his blazing speed caught up with the ball just as it was about to land. Another factor in the Dodgers' favor was that Amoros was a left-handed thrower and wore his glove on his right hand. Extending his glove to its fullest, he speared the ball just as it was about to drop and then turned and fired a strike to shortstop Reese, who relayed to first baseman Hodges, doubling up McDougald. Had Gilliam, a right-handed thrower, still been in left field, he would have had to reach across his body to backhand the ball and everyone agreed, there was no way he could have made the catch.

Podres then got Skowron on a ground ball to end the inning and keep the Yankees scoreless.

The Yankees put the tying runs on base again in the seventh, but Podres denied them once more, getting Berra on a soft fly to short right field and striking out Hank Bauer.

"I remember walking off the mound after I struck out Bauer and the crowd was going crazy," Podres said. "It seemed like everybody was a Dodgers fan. I said to myself, 'I can't let this game get away from me now.'"

He didn't. In the ninth, he got Skowron on a comebacker to the mound, Bob Cerv on a fly ball to left, and Elston Howard on a grounder to short. Podres had made good on his boast, a 2–0, eight-hit shutout, and the Dodgers had finally won the World Series, finally beaten the Yankees.

It was 1955, and, for the Dodgers, "next year" had arrived.

Bill Berens, left, walks dejectedly to the clubhouse after the Dodgers' Cookie Lavagetto spoiled his no-hitter in the 1947 World Series. That's a glum Joe DiMaggio on the right.

8. Cookie Monster

Many in the crowd of 33,443 could not grasp the full impact of what they were witnessing in Brooklyn's Ebbets Field on the afternoon of October 3, 1947. Going into the bottom of the ninth inning of Game 4 of the World Series, their Dodgers, already down two games to one in the Series, were trailing the Yankees by the score of 2–1.

But that was not the big story of the day.

What was being overlooked by most was that a journeyman Yankees pitcher, Floyd "Bill" Bevens, was only three outs away from doing what no pitcher in the history of baseball's showcase, the World Series, had ever done—pitch a no-hitter.

The reason it was overlooked was that over eight innings, Bevens, who had issued only 236 walks in 642 innings in his career, had walked eight batters in eight innings; had allowed a run in the fifth on two walks, a sacrifice, and a fielder's choice; and had pitched out of trouble in almost every inning.

Bevens was a 31-year-old right-hander from Hubbard, Oregon. Nothing in his background foretold he was capable of so lofty an accomplishment. He had come to the Yankees in 1944 and had posted a mediocre 40–36 record and pitched only six shutouts in four major league seasons.

In the 1947 regular season, Bevens was a disappointing 7–13, tied with two others for the fifth most wins among Yankees pitchers. He was not expected to be a factor in the World Series against the Dodgers, and yet here he was, flirting with history.

The Yankees had won the first two games at Yankee Stadium, a 5–3 victory in Game 1 with Frank "Spec" Shea and Joe Page combining on a six-hitter, and a 10–3 blowout in Game 2 behind Allie Reynolds's complete game.

The Dodgers bounced back in Game 3, outslugging the Yankees, 9–8, and now they were hoping to square the Series at two games apiece as Bevens opposed 10-game winner Harry Taylor. When the Yankees scored a run in the first and had the bases loaded with nobody out, Taylor was replaced by Hal Gregg, who pitched out of the jam without allowing another run and then kept the Dodgers close, allowing just one run over the next six innings.

Now, the Dodgers were three outs away from not only falling behind in the Series, three games to one, but suffering the added humiliation of being the first team to fail to get a hit in a World Series game.

To begin the bottom of the ninth, Bevens retired Bruce Edwards on a drive to deep left field, but the next batter, Carl Furillo, drew the erratic Bevens's ninth walk of the game to put the tying run on base.

Moments later, Bevens was only one out away from baseball history when he retired "Spider" Jorgensen on a pop foul to first baseman George McQuinn.

Dodgers manager Burt Shotton then made two critical and daring moves. He inserted speedy outfielder Al Gionfriddo as a pinch runner for Furillo and sent veteran Pete Reiser to the plate as a pinch-hitter for pitcher Hugh Casey.

Reiser was already a legend in Brooklyn baseball. As a youngster, he was possessed of blazing speed, awesome power, and all the attributes of a Hall of Famer. As a 21-year-old rookie in 1941, he led the National League in batting with a .343 average. His potential was unlimited until he was hampered by a series of injuries, including several concussions sustained by crashing into outfield walls that were unpadded in those days.

By 1947, Reiser was just a shell of his former self. Slowed by a second-half ankle injury, he had missed 44 games and batted .309 with only five home runs and 46 RBIs. He could hardly walk, let alone run, when he went to bat against Bevens, but he managed to conceal a perceptible limp when he went to the plate.

With Reiser at bat, Shotton's next daring move was to give Gionfriddo the steal sign. Had Gionfriddo been thrown out, the game would have ended and Bevens would have had his no-hitter, without Reiser getting a chance to swing the bat. But Gionfriddo slid in safely at second ahead of Yogi Berra's throw, putting the tying run in scoring position and keeping the Dodgers' hopes alive.

His reputation preceding him, Reiser still had the respect of opposing managers, including Yankees manager Bucky Harris, who daringly flew in the face of baseball's conventional wisdom by ordering an intentional walk to Reiser, thereby putting the winning run on base. Unable to run, Reiser was replaced at first base by pinch runner Eddie Miksis.

Scheduled to bat for the Dodgers was Eddie Stanky, known as "the Brat." Although he batted only .252 for the season, Stanky's reputation was that of a winner and a good performer in clutch situations, a player who would find a way to beat you.

Considering Stanky's reputation, Shotton's decision to replace him with pinch-hitter Cookie Lavagetto was a curious one.

Lavagetto was a veteran who had come to the Dodgers from Pittsburgh in 1937 and had been the Dodgers' regular third baseman for five seasons. Now 34 years old, he was reduced to a part-time player. He had played in only 41 games for the Dodgers in the 1947 season, 18 at third base, three at first base, and the remainder as a pinch-hitter. He had been to bat twice in the World Series without a hit, but he was about to experience the biggest moment in his career.

Lavagetto lifted a fly ball toward the short Ebbets Field right-field fence. Tommy Henrich, the Yankees' right fielder, moved back to the wall believing he would make the game-ending catch. To Henrich's surprise, the ball sailed over his head and slammed against the fence as first Gionfriddo, with the tying run, and then Miksis, with the winning run, came across home plate.

The Dodgers had won, 3–2, and evened the World Series at two games each. And Bevens trudged off the mound, not only a beaten pitcher, but denied his chance at baseball immortality.

As an ironic postscript to one of the most dramatic finishes ever in a World Series game, neither Bevens nor Lavagetto ever played another major league game.

9. The Pine-Tar Game

There was no love lost between George Brett and the Yankees to begin with. They had had their skirmishes before, but this time it erupted into full-scale war in Yankee Stadium on the afternoon of July 24, 1983.

This history of bad blood between Brett and the Yankees traced back almost a decade, all the way to the mid-1970s, when the Yankees and Brett's Kansas City Athletics met in three consecutive American League Championships Series in 1976, '77, and '78.

The Yankees won all three and Brett, an unrelenting competitor, bristled at his team's failure to make it to its first World Series.

In 1976, it was Brett's three-run home run in the top of the eighth inning of the deciding fifth game that tied the score, 6–6, and led to Yankee Chris Chambliss's dramatic, game-winning, and pennant-winning home run leading off the bottom of the ninth.

The following year, Brett was in the middle of hostilities as bad blood erupted on the playing field.

"We had a pretty good rivalry going," said Brett, "and there was some overaggressive play, almost to the point of being dirty. Hal McRae knocking Willie Randolph out in breaking up a double play, then laying on him and telling the guy from third base to score.

"Lou Piniella sliding into third base on a play where I didn't even have the ball. I was standing about three feet from the bag, and he came in and slid and tried to kick me with his spikes. That's the way the series was.

"Then, when I slid into third base Nettles kind of came up and threw a forearm and fell backwards a little," Brett recalled. "As I fell, Nettles stepped back and kicked me in the face. I got up and tried to throw punches."

It was both ugly and humorous to see the two premier American League third basemen rolling around on the ground and scuffling.

In 1978, the Yankees and Royals met again in the ALCS. With the series tied, one game each, Brett put on a show in Game 3 at Yankee Stadium. He belted three home runs, but the Yankees won the game, 6–5, and then took Game 4 to beat the Royals in the League Championship Series for the third straight year.

Brett would get his revenge two years later when the Yankees and Royals met in the ALCS for the fourth time in five years. Brett homered in Game 1, a 7–2 Kansas City victory, and his three-run homer off Goose Gossage in the seventh inning of Game 3 gave the Royals a 4–2 victory and a three-game sweep.

Now, five years later, the Yankees and Royals were meeting in Yankee Stadium with the Yankees in third place in the AL East, two games behind Toronto, and the Royals one game out in the AL West.

"When I was a kid, I wanted to do two things. Play major league baseball and be in the circus. I'm lucky, I got to do them both." —Graig Nettles, commenting on the constant turmoil surrounding the Yankees of the 1970s, known as "the Bronx Zoo"

The Yankees took a 4–3 lead into the top of the ninth. With two outs, U.L. Washington singled to keep the Royals' hopes alive, their best hitter, Brett, coming to bat as the go-ahead run. That brought Yankees manager Billy Martin to the mound to call for Gossage, baseball's most dominant closer at the time.

George Brett and an ump go head to head on July 24, 1983.

Brett turned on a Gossage fastball and drove it into the upper deck to give the Royals an apparent 5–4 lead. Brett circled the bases and returned to the Royals' dugout, where he sat down and noticed Martin at home plate, talking with plate umpire Tim McClelland. Suddenly, McClelland was headed for the Royals' dugout, asking to inspect Brett's bat.

McClelland carried the bat to home plate, where he conferred with the umpiring crew. Moments later, McClelland thrust his right arm in the air and called Brett out for excessive use of pine tar on his bat, citing baseball rule 1.10 (b), to wit: "A bat may not be covered by such a substance more than 18 inches from the tip of the handle."

By laying the bat against home plate, which is 17 inches wide, McClelland determined that Brett's bat had pine tar 19 to 20 inches from the tip of the handle and lighter pine tar for another three or four inches. He nullified the home run and called Brett out, giving the Yankees a 4–3 victory.

With that, Brett went ballistic. He was a man gone wild, charging out of the Royals' dugout after McClelland, and had to be restrained by Royals players and coaches.

Later, Martin explained that the Yankees had noticed in an earlier game that Brett was using a bat with excessive pine tar. Nettles pointed out the infraction to Martin, who chose not to make an issue of it at the time.

"You don't call him on it if he makes an out," said Martin. "We waited until he did something to beat us. After he hit the home run, I remembered what Nettles told me, and I went out and said he's using an illegal bat."

The Royals protested the game, and it was left to American League president Lee MacPhail to rule on the protest. After hearing arguments from the Royals and Yankees and discussing the matter with the umpires, MacPhail overturned the umpire's decision and ordered the game resumed on August 18, a common day off for both teams, at the point following Brett's home run with the Royals leading, 5–4.

Acknowledging that Brett had pine tar too high on his bat, McPhail cited "the spirit of the rule," and his belief that "games should be won and lost on the playing field, not through technicalities of the rules."

Only a few hundred showed up in Yankee Stadium on August 18 for the completion of a game that had started 25 days before.

It took 12 minutes and 16 pitches for the issue to be decided.

When the Yankees took the field for the final out in the top of the ninth, Ron Guidry, a pitcher, was in center field, and Don Mattingly, a left-handed thrower, was at second base. Neither was needed, however, as McRae struck out to end the inning.

In the bottom of the ninth, Dan Quisenberry faced three batters and retired them all.

The Royals had won the game, 5–4, and George Brett had the last laugh.

Grover Cleveland Alexander of the Cards and Bob Shawkey of the Yankees, opposing pitchers shake hands before Game 6 of the 1926 World Series.

10. Alexander the Great

Old Pete's work was finished, he had done his job, and that was enough of a reason for a night on the town. It was a special night, and a special town. New York, the city that never sleeps, and Old Pete, who believed sleep was a waste of time. A perfect match!

Grover Cleveland Alexander, the man they called "Old Pete," had pitched the St. Louis Cardinals to a 10–2 victory over the New York Yankees in Game 6 of the 1926 World Series, his second complete-game victory in six days. He had pitched his team into a seventh game, a chance to win their first World Series ever, and he figured all he would have to do the next day was sit back and watch it happen.

Old Pete was four months short of his 40th birthday, an alcoholic, an epileptic, and partially deaf, a consequence of serving with the artillery in France in 1918 in the first great "war to end all wars."

"It's great to be young and a Yankee." —Hall of Famer Waite Hoyt, at age 27 in 1927, after leading the American League with 22 victories

Alexander was one of the great pitchers, and great characters, of baseball's "dark ages"–so great a character that Hollywood immortalized him in a movie of his life, *The Winning Team*, with Ronald Reagan playing the part of Alexander.

The Phillies had purchased Alexander's contract from Syracuse of the International League for $750 in 1911. As a rookie, he led the National League with 28 victories, 31 complete games, 367 innings, and seven shutouts.

Over the next several years, he would win 30 or more games in three straight seasons, lead the league in wins four times, in earned-run average three times, in strikeouts five times, in complete games four times, in innings pitched five times, and in shutouts four times, including a still-standing record of 16 in 1916. And he would vie with the Giants' Christy Mathewson for the distinction of being the National League's best pitcher.

Despite his 30 wins for the Phillies in 1917, Alexander was traded to the Cubs the next season, went off to war, but returned to continue being a dominant pitcher. When Joe McCarthy took over as Cubs manager and grew impatient with Alex's off-field behavior, he dealt him to the Cardinals for the $6,000 waiver price.

When he joined the Cardinals on June 22, 1926, Alexander was 39 years old and had won 328 major league games (he would finish with 373 wins, tied with Mathewson for second place on the all-time list behind Cy Young).

Alexander's nine wins and veteran presence no doubt was the difference in the Cardinals' winning their first pennant, by two games over Cincinnati.

The Cardinals were decided underdogs in the World Series against the powerhouse Yankees of Babe Ruth, Lou Gehrig, Tony Lazzeri, and Bob Meusel.

After Herb Pennock outpitched Bill Sherdel to take Game 1, 2–1, Alexander got the call from manager Rogers Hornsby in the second game. Old Pete was on his game against the powerful Yankees. He held Ruth, Gehrig, Meusel, and Lazzeri to two harmless singles in 14 at-bats, allowed four hits, struck out 10, and retired the last 21 batters to even the Series with a 6–2 victory.

The Yankees and Cardinals split the next two games, and the Yanks won Game 5 in St. Louis, 3–2, when Alexander's turn came up again. It was up to him to force a seventh game and give the Cardinals a chance. In order to win the World Series, the Cardinals were going to have to sweep the last two games in Yankee Stadium.

Again, Alex held the mighty Babe Ruth hitless, pitched another complete game, and beat the Yankees in Game 6, 10–2, thanks to a 13-hit barrage by his Cardinals teammates.

The pitching pairing for the deciding game was 16-game winner Waite Hoyt, the winner of Game 4, for the Yankees, against 13-game winner Jesse Haines, the winner of Game 3, for the Cardinals, a matchup that favored the Yankees playing at home.

Ruth's fourth home run of the Series (he had hit three in Game 4), gave the Yankees a 1–0 lead in the third. But the Yanks' defense betrayed Hoyt in the fourth, allowing the Cardinals to score three unearned runs for a 3–1 lead.

The Yankees scored a run in the sixth, and then, with Haines bothered by a blister on the index finger of his pitching hand, the Yankees rallied in the seventh. When Gehrig walked with two outs, the Yankees had the bases loaded and Lazzeri coming to bat.

Hornsby went to the mound to replace Haines and called for Alexander, which surprised not only the crowd but Old Pete himself, who was battling a hangover from his revelry of the previous night.

With the count 1–1, Alexander threw a pitch in Lazzeri's happy zone, and Lazzeri gave it a ride, a line drive down the left-field line. The ball whistled into the seats, foul by inches.

Given a second chance, Old Pete reared back and put everything he had behind his next pitch, a fastball. Lazzeri swung and missed, and the Cardinals' 3–2 lead was preserved.

The Yankees had two more cracks at Alexander, and Ruth would get another at-bat.

In the eighth, Alexander retired "Jumping" Joe Dugan, Pat Colllins, and Pennock in order.

In the ninth, Old Pete faced the top of the Yankees' batting order. Earle Combs grounded to third. Mark Koenig also grounded to third. That brought up the mighty Babe Ruth, who had blasted 47 home runs during the season and four more in the World Series. The count went to 3–2. Pitching carefully, Alexander misfired with his next pitch and Ruth trotted to first base with his 11th walk of the Series.

The Yankees' next batter was Meusel, the big slugger who had doubled and tripled earlier in the game. For some strange, inexplicable reason, Ruth decided, on his own, and with Meusel at bat, to take off for second base. Catcher Bob O'Farrell gunned the ball to second baseman Hornsby, who slapped the tag on Ruth for the final out.

The World Series was over, the Cardinals were champs, and Old Pete, Grover Cleveland Alexander, was the unlikely hero.

A capacity crowd on a summer day at
Yankee Stadium

Reggie Jackson and manager Billy Martin of the Yanks won the World Series by defeating the Los Angeles Dodgers 8–4 in the sixth game.

New York Yankees owner George Steinbrenner (left)
and Manager Yogi Berra in the dugout on the first
day of spring training.

Joe Torre, manager of the New York Yankees, signs autographs for fans prior to a spring training game on March 10, 2007 at McKechnie Field in Bradenton, Florida.

Derek Jeter sprays fans with champagne after the Yankees defeated the Atlanta Braves 4–1 to win the World Series.

New York Yankees Hall of Fame player
Yogi Berra (right) reacts as team manager
Joe Torre presents him with a 1998 World
Series ring during Yogi Berra Day.